CW00432217

GOALS for GALILEE

GOALS for GALILEE

The Triumphs and Traumas of The Sons of Sakhnin, Israel's Arab Football Club

JERROLD KESSEL AND PIERRE KLOCHENDLER

BOOKS

First published in Great Britain in 2010 by
JR Books, 10 Greenland Street, London NW1 0ND
www.jrbooks.com

Copyright © 2010 Jerrold Kessel and Pierre Klochendler

Jerrold Kessel and Pierre Klochendler have asserted their moral right to be
identified as the Authors of this Work in accordance with the Copyright
Designs and Patents Act 1988.

All rights reserved. No part of this book may be reproduced or utilised in any
form or by any means, electronic or mechanical, including photocopying,
recording or by any information storage and retrieval system, without
permission in writing from JR Books.

A catalogue record for this book is available from the British Library.

ISBN 978-1-906217-43-3

1 3 5 7 9 10 8 6 4 2

Printed by MPG Books, Bodmin, Cornwall

Contents

For the people of Sakhnin
For The Sons of Sakhnin

Acknowledgements

Goals for Galilee is the fruit of several seasons in which we followed the fluctuating fortunes of The Sons of Sakhnin. We would never have been able to tell their story without the warm embrace of the people of Sakhnin, of the fans of Sakhnin, and of The Sons themselves. We are grateful for that.

Our special thanks go to the Goals for Galilee XI, our main source of inspiration: goalie – the Sakhnin stadium; defenders – Ghazal Abu Raya, Mundar Haleileh, Mazen Ghanaim and Ibrahim Bushnaq; mid-fielders – Taysir Hasqiyah, Abbas Suan, and Abdallah Ghanaim; strikers – Mahmoud Ghalia, Eyal Lachman and Wurrod Miari; manager – Mohammed Bashir (Abu Shadi); coach – Mohammed Hayadry (Abu Majdi); bench – Hilmi Bushnaq, Safa Suan, Sa'id Hamad, Suan and the whole Suan family; cheerleader – Gumbul; and finally the Abu Ali Restaurant and Walid Hamzeh Bros. Bakery, both of which provided real food for thought.

Warm thanks to our agent Deborah Harris and her assistant Ines Austern who, from the very beginning, believed in the book and understood the importance of the story, and to Jeremy

Robson and his staff at JR Books, who have now made it happen.

Goals for Galilee is the story of the Big Match – Jewish majority v Arab minority in Israel – an elemental season, and a season of survival. We wish Sakhnin not just survival – but many seasons full of triumph and many more trophies.

We engaged with Sakhnin not only using a pencil, but also with a camera. Prior to writing the book, we had published a long series of articles, 'The World According to Sakhnin', in the Tel Aviv newspaper, *Haaretz*, and also made a documentary film, *We Too Have No Other Land*. For those opportunities in helping us conceptualise our thoughts, we are grateful to our friend and colleague David Landau, the *Haaretz* editor-in-chief, Ruth Diskin, the distributor of our documentary, and Itay Landsberg of the Israeli Broadcasting Authority, which helped co-produce the film.

With *Goals for Galilee*, we hope to have somehow squared the Sakhnin soccer saga into one round ball.

Finally, our warmest thanks go to our families: to Lorraine, Ariel and Michal Kessel, and Yael Abessira for their constant support through this experience; and to Roi and Ori Diamant, Shai-Li Kessel, and Yasmine, Solal and Miryam Klochendler for joining the Sakhnin fans at some of the games. We hope that somehow, sometime, not too many seasons down the line, they will be able to celebrate, along with the sons and daughters of The Sons, the real Sakhnin goal – a draw between majority and minority.

Chapter 1

The First and Last Time I Saw the Cup

National Stadium, Ramat Gan

TAYSIR HASQIYAH NEVER misses a Bnei Sakhnin game. Why do you come to the games, I always get asked. For the record, for the umpteenth time, it's all because of Mazen, our chairman Mazen Ghanaim. There's a man who knows not just the power of words, but how to deliver them. Every time he's up against a venomous question about Jews and Arabs he pulls the snake out of the hole and slings it off the pitch: There's no hatred around our games, and much of that is down to how true and straight Mazen speaks. He makes everybody feel good, not just us. He makes the world of soccer pure and simple: there are only supporters or non-supporters — that's the only distinction. In my view, we're all supporters, Jews and Arabs. Until Mazen became famous and they began to interview him on

1

the radio, I used to follow my Sons and watch all their games on TV. But the moment I heard him talking, I told myself, Taysir, *yallah* let's go! I just had to be there with him and my brothers, at the ground, to watch The Sons.

I'm from Tira. In case you don't know, that's a small town 20 miles north-east of Tel Aviv near the pre-1967 Green Line border with the West Bank. We're one of several small Arab-Israeli towns or large villages – town, village, it all depends on how the taxman thinks it's in his interest to define us. We're part of the area we in Israel call the 'Small Triangle' – Tira-Taibeh-Kfar Qassem – as distinct from the 'Large Triangle', the one formed by our Palestinian neighbours with their three corner towns on the West Bank – Jenin-Nablus-Tulkarm.

I may be from a small triangle but when it comes to soccer and me, there's nothing small about me. And I'm not only talking about my belly. In soccer, thanks to Sakhnin, I live big. Fervent isn't the word. I own up to 'fanatic'. Actually, fanatic isn't the word either. There's no word to describe Taysir Hasqiyah and soccer. At least, none I'm aware of in Arabic or in Hebrew. Not even in Mazen's language. No wonder people are always teasing me – what's with you Taysir, every game, every Saturday, rain or scorching sun? Still, they ask me – why on earth would a blind man come to games, even this game?

So what if I'm blind. Am I going to miss all this just because I can't see, I tell them. Are you silly? Anyway, they can't see that I can't see. I always wear my sunglasses.

That day we won the Cup, that night, that victory was something else altogether. You didn't need to be a fanatic to have wanted to be there. You didn't have to see to feel that this was history-in-the-making. I still get goose pimples even now, and

I'm no softie. You can't imagine the feeling of togetherness.

Strange to think back now and to realise that, although our opponents in the final, Hapoel Haifa, were in the second division and we were in the premier league, we were considered the underdogs. It makes sense, I suppose, because we're Arabs, the sons of the minority. You wouldn't think it made sense because Haifa also had three Arab players in their starting line-up and one of them was even a Sakhnin boy. But that didn't matter. They're not an Arab club, we are, and this was going to be our big night, and no one was going to rob us of it – not even a few lousy Arabs.

I knew that.

We all knew that.

True, some faint-hearted types began to show their doubts when the opening whistle blew. But they were faint-hearted types. I'd organised seven buses packed with kids and teenagers whose families couldn't afford tickets. I fixed it that they could all go. No one should've been allowed to miss that night. I had a loudspeaker fixed on top of the lead bus in the Tira convoy. We first headed north before driving south to Ramat Gan ('Hey, Taysir, you're taking us the wrong way!') just so that we could drive up and down the road before we made for the stadium ('okay, that makes sense'). Ramat Gan, formally a town on its own, but everyone knows it's really part of the Tel Aviv metropolis. I was the muezzin summoning the faithful: People of Galilee! Kick-off's in four hours! Time to hit the road! Don't miss the match of our lives! Cup Final night tonight: Bnei Sakhnin versus Hapoel Haifa. Don't be late! Don't let The Sons down!

Inside the National Stadium, there's another muezzin in full cry. There's no way I can steal the thunder of the Gumbul Trio. That Gumbul – he's master of the drums, king of the *darbuka*, conductor of the fans. On one hand, I'm happy I'm here behind the goal and not near Gumbul there in those fancy seats on the half-way line. I'd be deaf by now. But, on the other, I don't have the best of views from down here. I don't get the game in stereo. I wish I'd brought my transistor radio to get the return feed of the match commentary. But hell, what do I need my radio for tonight? I know how to watch a Sakhnin game. And I know we're going to win. And I'll have the last laugh over Gumbul. All the night's five goals will be scored at our end – right between our eyes.

We all cheered loudly for the FA, who had the good sense to send a troop of kids to parade around the pitch with banners heralding 'The War Against Racism and Violence in Sport'. We even cheered when the Israeli army band played a military march and the State President made his run-on. Gumbul was at full throttle: left–right, left–right, you could hear him marshalling the band and the President. I told you it was our night. Suddenly, his drums faded. It took me a second to work out that the army band was playing the national anthem. Sensibly, everyone kept quiet, waiting patiently for *Hatikvah* to be over so we could get down to the real business of tonight. But it was fun that they played it for us. All the Arab towns were there.

At first, the game was pretty even. As if The Sons didn't want to dispel our underdog tag. That would've been presumptuous. You don't lose your underdog status just because you play Haifa in the Cup Final. That'd be going overboard. Maybe they were just nervous. You could tell they were. I wasn't, but they were. I never doubted them for a minute. Except when there was an obvious foul down at the other end – everybody saw it, a definite Sakhnin penalty, but that man in black shorts, he wouldn't give it, he was obviously out to spoil things – what's he trying to be, the death of our hopes, you miserable ref? You want us to stay underdogs forever? Over my dead body! He didn't let up, that man in black. He should've blown for the half long before. That's why Haifa got their goal right there, in front of me, in injury time! I felt I was facing a firing squad. Bear the torture, my friend. The joy will be even greater. And guess who scored? Shai Dahan. May that dastardly son-of-a-bitch's father's chest bone be cursed! What does he think he's doing? He used to play for us, the rat.

At last, black shorts blows: half-time.

Oi–yoi–yoi!

Ai–yai–yai!

Men, women, children, to a man – they were weeping. An Arab doesn't cry, I scold them. We're coming home with the Cup, with the State Cup, remember. I say Ramat Gan will speak Arabic tonight. I had to buck them up lest, on the strength of all the weeping and wailing that's going on around me, the Haifa goalie is going to make a few damned saves. This half, he's going to be in earshot, right here beneath us. I want to hear him weeping.

Desperate action was needed. So, I started singing the song which had been buzzing in my head all week long. I needed to convince all those wimps that my predictions would all come true:

Yo–yo–yo!
Yeh–yeh–yeh!
Sakhnin, Sakhnin, Sakhnin!
We salute you, O Sakhnin,
Mighty cup holders,
Mighty red stallions.

Bnei Sakhnin, Sons United
Yo–yo-yo!
Yeh-yeh-yeh!
Every ball's our gaoler's –
Proud custodian
Of our goal.
No ball gets by Komiko Kamara –
Multi-lock Son of Sakhnin!
Yo–yo-yo!
Yeh-yeh-yeh!
Hapoel Haifa –
We give you naught,
Have them eat grass.
Asulin, Lima – Asulima!
With them, we eat honey.

It worked. They began joining the chant: Yo–yo-yo! Yeh-yeh-yeh! My calm was spreading. I'd already ploughed through a whole pack of Marlboros. Usually, I make do with just half-a-pack a half.

Second half. Here they are, right on time. Give me one of your fags, I've run out. My neighbour grabs the new pack. He's frantic. 'Bibo' Avi Danan, the Beit Shean son of Bnei Sakhnin, the central pole of The Sons' defence, is pushing forward. Long as he gets back to defend in time. Long live Avi! He's won a corner. Asulin takes it rather than Abbas. Avi's possessed. He gets his head through a cluster of heads. He heads it home. Hallelujah! *Zagruta*, as we say in Arabic. The equaliser at last! 62nd minute – blessed art thou! Applause, cries, hugs. A total stranger throws his arms around me and plants a big kiss on my brow. Welcome, welcome, help yourself, don't be shy, no one's a stranger tonight. More crying. Still half-an-hour to go. Plenty of time for more, I tell them.

When will the next come?

Soon, soon I tell you, soon.

When soon?

Soon – now, this very second.

And, the second: Lior Asulin, king of the net! I'm lifted off my feet. Easy, easy, calm down guys, I'm trying to follow the game. What'll you do when we score the third?

When?

Soon.

Everyone's fainting around me. A guy falls in my arms. I remonstrate: Let's watch the game, for heaven's sake. This is no time for the faint-hearted. It's time for us to keep our nerve. He comes round. I reassure him: Still, two fingers to one.

That second goal sent me off to the kiosk behind the stands. Gimme a bottle. Mineral water, please. I may be hot-blooded but I'm super-cool at living the game. I order a cup of coffee. I tell Ahmad my boy – he was 10 then – you want a popsicle? Here's some money, take. It's in the bag, son, we can go home. We're coming home with the Cup.

Yo–yo-yo!

Yeh-yeh-yeh!

I'm back at my post. That guy next to me, he's still not calm, he still can't believe. He can't take it. He's still smoking my fags. Unbeatable Komiko saves again. The man in black shows Asulin a yellow. Asulin king of yellows, my Jewish hero! But here's our angel Gabriel, Gabriel Lima. He dribbles, passes, gallops, flies round the goalie.

7

Sakhnin, Br–aaa–ziiilllll!

Yo–yo-yo!

Yeh-yeh-yeh!

3-1.

I'm totally under control. I get kicked on the head. A father has just thrown his son (his real son) so high into the air he's never going to land back from heaven. But he does. On my bald head. *Allahu akbar*, God's greatest! Calm? You can't get any calmer. I sing, I yell, I'm going berserk. What's happening to you, Taysir? You're crying like you've never cried in your life before. I've never had a chance to cry like this before.

PENALTY! I hear the yells.

Now, I'm really being put to the test.

Thank God, it's to us, I'm told. The ref has awarded it to us.

C'mon Abbas, make it four! Ab-bas Su-uan! He'll lift us high. Abbas, star of stars.

Captain of the eastern star. Abbas, my soul!

Asulin's so fired up he wants another goal. Again, he's grabbed the ball from Abbas. Let Abbas take it. Our king never misses. I don't want to curse you, Asulin. He scores. Asulin, prince of Sakhnin! 88th minute: blessed art thou. 4-1. Now, I'm optimistic, I'm confident, surely we can't lose now. Can we? Everyone's calming down and I'm getting all jumpy. Injury time. Blow already, blow, you white angel in black shorts. Don't spoil the party at the last minute. It's our Cup. What a night, what a game, I don't want it to end. The white angel, blessed be he, finally he blows. Our Sons are mobbing one another. We could've jumped the fence to join them. We held back. We know our place. Still, there are enough people mobbing Abbas. When he gets the trophy from the State President, he has to be lifted onto a pyramid of shoulders to lift it high enough to show it off to us. How it gleams, my neighbour tells me. Tell me about it, tell me again, I tell him. I can feel it – it gleams in my heart. The players are showered with red-and-white confetti. Our colours. I hear my neighbour gasp. Other colours have joined the melee – the blue-and-white of Israel. From somewhere in the stands, who knows from where – from someone in the stands, who knows from whom – Asulin has conjured up a national flag. He wraps it around his shoulders like the prayer shawl with which our Jewish brothers cover themselves in their prayers. He twirls the flag joyously and does a victory lap of honour and we honour him: As-su-lin! As-su-lin! You're red, red's your colour. Tonight, Ramat Gan speaks Arabic.

I've lost my shirt. Lucky it's a warm night. Who cares what we look like? I was just leaving the ground when I bump into this young Jewish guy going out of Gate 13. I press him into doing a jig with me. He's a bit put out. You ask how I knew he was Jewish? Precisely because he's put out. He tells me I'm put out, I'm a Haifa fan. I tell him we're all one family now – Jews, Arabs, Haifa, Sakhnin, as long as you're a supporter. We're all in it together. He hugs me. I'm happy for your happiness, he tells me. He's happy now too. I'm happy you're happy, I tell him back. Boy, were we happy! We weep together. Ahmad's astonished. I can feel him looking at me wide-eyed – he's never seen his dad laughing and crying and kissing a Jewish guy all at the same time. I'm good at that – doing three different things at the same time.

We set off home. Forget Tira, son. Sakhnin is home now. We're Sakhnin now. Son, *Ich bin ein Sakhniner*, as I say in the Kennedy language I know. About two after midnight, we finally reach Sakhnin, Sakhnin my soul! Some of my friends take their little kids to bed. Ahmad and I stay in the main road, singing and dancing all night. Fireworks too. It's Sakhnin's night of independence. Mazen brings out the Cup. Everyone goes berserk again. A night like that – it's once in a lifetime. We deserved four cups, I tell you, not one.

That's the last time we saw the Cup, our Cup of independence.

Chapter 2

New Season, New Adventures

Downtown Sakhnin

OW LONG CAN we live on that night, for goodness sake? Ibrahim, watch out! A hooter. And another. Rasping Arabic rap music belches out from a car radio and rocks the little roundabout that feeds traffic into downtown Sakhnin where Main Street and al-Aqsa Martyrs' Street intersect. The rap trails away in the smoking exhaust. Sakhnin — gateway to soccer heaven! But, before the gates of heaven, there's a whole life to be lived — a life of tension poised between lasting failures and ephemeral success. Many things may hinder a full soccer life. There are many impediments on the road to achieving what's expected in life — to win as much as possible. How to make the most of the tension?

Wurrod Miari is shepherding her bunch of eight-year-olds back to her classroom. They've been visiting an exhibition of painting by children from neighbouring towns: If you've never known failure, you'll never know victory. Quick, quick. Hanan, mind that van! Wurrod guides her pupils through the chaotic streets. A lorry screeches to a belated halt near the roundabout. A tractor pulls up from the other side. The drivers get grateful nods from the teacher: See, there's nowhere to cross. It's such a busy road, yet no traffic lights, no proper pedestrian crossing. There's nothing in Sakhnin, nothing, only soccer.

A tightrope through life.

Wurrod's in her early 30s. We've come across her and her brood entirely by accident when we came to a belated halt ourselves near the roundabout. Then a breathless monologue on the run: Nothing, nothing, nothing, that's what we have here. That's our lives here. Marwa, don't run, I tell you! Keep your head, will you, get out of the street! An alarmed hooter. At the last second, she pulls another stray chick out of the way of a passing minibus. We have to beat the nothing, to beat the impossible. We have to make it all possible. And, if we believe in ourselves, we'll make lots possible. We'll make a revolution – not only in Sakhnin, but in the whole world.

The school gates beckon. Innocence and experience breathe fast together on the sharp little hill, innocence battles experience for first place home. The Star of David of the blue-and-white national flag flutters atop the main school building under a mild wind. 'Wadi Safa Elementary School, Sakhnin' is recorded perfunctorily in both Arabic and Hebrew on a plaque on the side of the two-storey limestone block. Wurrod tumbles on: Maybe we'll lose, maybe we'll win, I dunno. Only God knows – goodness, let me breathe, give me a break! Her chuckle interrupts the flow.

Questions are out of the question. No dialogue, no

prompting. Uncensored passion. Straight from the heart. First-class soccer philosophy. All in a day's work for a standard-one teacher: Here's our school. Several little girls take up the cheer. They jump with delight: Yeah, yeah, yeah! They're so happy that you're here. You're the first outsiders to come here, the first to really want to know about us. At the sky-blue iron gates: *Ahlanwa-sahlanbikum* – a warm welcome to you.

Home of The Sons

Welcome to The Sons of Sakhnin – Cinderellas in soccer boots!

When Mazen Ghanaim, the chairman of the town's football club, greets visitors, he unfailingly quotes Bill Shankly about football being more important than life and death: We know we're no match for Mr. Shankly's great club. But we are The Sons of Sakhnin, the sons of Israel's million point two Arabs. We live our football. We match anyone in the world in our passion. We're entitled to tell our soccer brethren in northern England: Eat your hearts out, Liverpool – we are Sakhnin!

The town used to have two small clubs, Maccabi Sakhnin and Hapoel Sakhnin. They were great rivals. In 1996, taking the names Ihud (Hebrew: United) and Bnei (Hebrew: Sons of), the clubs merged. Hapoel Ihud Bnei Sakhnin was born.

The club's stock began to rise. In 2003, for the first time, Sakhnin gained promotion to Israel's top tier of competitive football. There was a downside though. Since the small run-down municipal stadium was deemed unfit for use in the Premier League, The Sons lost the use of their home ground. Yet, remarkably, in their inaugural season in the top flight, not only did the little-fancied team from the Galilee avoid relegation, they won the State Cup – the equivalent of the FA Cup – and in doing so won a place to represent Israeli soccer in the UEFA Cup.

The Sons' Cup triumph put the town of 25,000 on the national pitch. The Israeli government was committed to helping Sakhnin to complete its new ground. But, for Sakhnin's mayor, Mohammed Bashir (Abu Shadi), the challenge goes way beyond football: For us, it's a mega match, 'The Mother of All Matches', majority v minority. The land is our pitch, and our goal this season is to convince the Jewish majority that what we, the Arab minority, seek is to become part of this country. We want to convince them that equality comes not just by playing together, definitely not by tackling or kicking each other, but by understanding each other.

Mundar Haleileh, the club spokesman, takes up the pass: A society is best judged by how it relates to its minority within its midst. We are by law full citizens of Israel, and our political parties represent us in Israel's parliament, the Knesset. We're 20 per cent of the country, yet we're still in the relegation zone of Israeli society. When we challenge that politically, it's so easy to fob us off. The response is mistrust and resistance to change. Now, finally, with our Cup, which we owe to no one but ourselves, we've earned respect and an alternative platform from which to win over the hearts of our Jewish brothers to score the goal politicians have failed to score – equality.

Can football bring the Arabs of Israel centre-pitch alongside the Jews of Israel? Can the two together square the cardinal issues of identity, discrimination, equality, acceptance and coexistence into the one round ball?

Big asks for football!

'Home' to Tirana and Beersheba

Playing Partizani Tirana of Albania in suburban Tel Aviv doesn't really have the trappings of a genuine global adventure. Still, it's the UEFA Cup second qualifying round and it's the National Stadium and, it's Sakhnin's first venture into the global village – two 'home' games, in fact, from village to globe and back to village. 'Historic game' is bandied about on every corner of Sakhnin. Maybe not historic, but a real 'first' – the first time any Arab club is in any European competition. An Arab first, thanks to Israel. Thanks to Arab politics, Israel is barred from playing against the Arab world. Thanks to Europe, Israel thus plays in Europe. And it doesn't matter that the opening game is against a team from a country with a rather dubious 'world's most' title: Sakhnin may be on the sidelines of Israel, but Albania is still tackling its legacy of decades as the world's most secluded state.

We're all Albanians! Sakhnin spokesman Ghazal Abu Raya is a sort of mediaeval town crier. He heralds this opening European bout as 'A Third-World derby' or 'Third-World Albania versus Third-World town Sakhnin played in First-World Israel'. By playing up glaring inequalities, Ghazal's not entirely fair to any of the three teams involved. After all, on the soccer field, no one wants to be a cry-baby, to have their weaknesses exposed before kick-off.

Superintendent Shimon, a policeman on duty outside the ground, isn't worried, just slightly patronising: This won't be a difficult game for us, the crowd will be small. He's backed up by the manager of the National Stadium, Yablo Yablkovsky: Never has my ground been so empty. World-class grass, what a waste! Barely 3,000 are here – 39,000 colourful plastic seats bare of bums.

Still, the many families who've come from Galilee create a homely atmosphere. There's some choice Arabic, especially when Arabic-speaking players try something beyond them: Who the hell do you think you are, Abed Rabbah – Real Madrid? Roberto Carlos? The full-back's attempt at a 40-yard first-timer ends up pitifully near the corner flag. But in between the Arabic, the jolly singing is all in Hebrew, an adaptation of a classic Israeli tune:

Hop-Hop-Hop,

Sakhnin in Europe!

An awful lot of people are trying hard to load an awful lot of baggage onto the slender shoulders of the team from Galilee. Sakhnin – 'hotbed of Palestinian nationalist sentiment,' they used to say – almost a national mantra among Jewish Israelis. Now, that's become Sakhnin 'symbol of Arab-Jewish coexistence', 'bridge to peace', 'fount of intercommunal fraternity.' You can read anything you want into Sakhnin.

The mantras are headlines in the Tel Aviv tabloids, and not only on the sports pages. One day, it's a story that the Foreign Ministry in Jerusalem 'intends to exploit the Sakhnin players as unofficial ambassadors' in order to promote Israel's cause in Europe. On another, it's that a PLO man in Tirana is drumming up 'Arab support' to show solidarity for The Sons when they travel to Albania for the return leg in a fortnight's time. Ibrahim Bushnaq, Sakhnin's foreign liaison man, is unimpressed on both counts: We're not involved in any of this – our business is football, full stop. A diplomat's answer.

Impeccably dressed, fluent in English, man-of-the-world Ibrahim knows all too well when Sakhnin needs to sound 'soccerly correct'. In Sakhnin parlance, it's damned politically incorrect to tell outsiders that their business is more than soccer. But haven't we just read in the Sakhnin match programme that that's precisely what Sakhnin's soccer is – much more than soccer. That for Sakhnin, winning means much more than winning a league game or winning a cup – that it's bound up with winning over the majority, with 'settling in the hearts of the majority'. They walk a thin line – between how to play their soccer 'message', the 'value' of their soccer, and the kind of results they want out of their soccer success.

There's clearly something to this positive spin. Identity is not the only stimulus for loyalty. Geography also breeds soccer loyalty. Among the Sakhnin faithful that night are two young fellows with rucksacks who're asking how do we get to Armoured Corps House after the game? They need a bed for the night. They're doing army service and their home is in Carmiel, the Jewish town in Galilee over the hill from Sakhnin. They're literally our neighbourhood team, they say, it's natural we support them rather than one of the big clubs in Haifa or Tel Aviv.

Still, there's a mystery why Sakhnin hasn't been able to draw a much larger crowd for this 'historic match'. The chairman offers a down-to-earth explanation: Several weddings were scheduled in Sakhnin for this particular evening, so many townsfolk who would have come, couldn't. It's all in the family. Sometimes a village can't play to the tune of the global game. But what about The Sons' fans from other Arab towns and villages? Where are Taysir's coaches bringing Tira, Taibeh, Nazareth, Kfar Kana to the National Stadium? Maybe it's not Cup Final night, but doesn't Mazen declare over and over that The Sons proudly represent not just Israel in Europe, but also all the million-plus non-Jewish citizens in Israel?

That doesn't automatically mean they've been elected to do so by the other 1,175,000-odd who don't live in Sakhnin – especially when proximity's a cause of soccer, or family, rivalry. Take The Sons' neighbours, for instance, the Brothers of Nazareth – Ahi Nazeret – the country's other top Arab club. Such deadly rivalry isn't easily set aside: Just because Sakhnin are now the most famous club team in all the Middle East? Just because they think they're representing Israel, all Israel, including us, Nazareth, the country's biggest Arab town? It's clearly not at all clear that the Nazarene Bros. see eye to eye with Sakhnin about The Sons assuming the role of representing Israel on their behalf.

It's not that Bnei Sakhnin hasn't done its level best to attract a much bigger following. One way is to recruit good foreign players. On first showing, manager Eyal Lachman has brought in quite a classy bunch this season, five players from Africa and Brazil. He's managed to convince them that faith leads to Galilee and that world success starts in Galilee. The modest hero of tonight's game is Nigerian Agoye Olomide: I've been here only a couple of months but I feel like I've been here forever, that this is home. The welcome has been as warm as that. This was my way of paying something back.

Payback in style – this evening. True, Abbas had eased any nerves with an early goal, but then Agoye scored the other two in a famous victory. Payback, money – it was certainly a factor in his decision to move to the Middle East. What of the lofty ideals which Sakhnin is being told to fulfil? He echoes Ibrahim: Tell you the truth, I play football, the identity of people doesn't matter one bit. Then he remembers this isn't just any ordinary 3-0 victory. He needs to say something to suit the role The Sons are mapping out: This club is busy making history, and I would like to be part of that.

Nice ambition, nice thought. But it can't last all season, can it? Can't it?

Yes, it can!

The answer comes nine days later at Illut stadium outside Nazareth where, in the absence of their home stadium, Bnei Sakhnin are contracted to play this season's National League fixtures. Hapoel Beersheba are the visitors. As with the start of any league season, it's an exhilarating moment. Anything's possible. Everything's possible:

This is going to be the best winning season of our lives. We have a very good team and all the Arabs of Israel are behind us.

And the Arabs of Palestine?

Them too. If they could come to support us and what we are trying to do, we think they would.

No one wants to be drawn on whether Sakhnin shouldn't feel closer still to the Arab world. Many are still smarting from the fact that, as Israelis, they've been barred from participating in the pan-Arab 'A Star Is Born' TV talent contest which, for the last few weeks, has been rocking the whole Arab world. For the rest of the Arab world, Sakhnin's status as a 'soccer star is born' is something of a double-edged sword. They simply don't want to play ball with the Israeli Cup holders. That leaves The Sons with an Arab world that isn't altogether round.

Before kick-off, the watchwords of coexistence, peace, communal fraternity are trumpeted here, there, everywhere, by officials and fans alike. At kick-off, one fan declines to give his identity and agrees to talk only on condition of anonymity. He doesn't hold back on his tackle: I love Sakhnin, I l-o-v-e them. I want . . . I want . . . I want so much to beat the Jews from

Beersheba, from Haifa, from Tel Aviv! At last, we have a real chance of doing so.

The man in charge of Illut is a Brothers' fan, a Nazarene through and through, and he makes sure everyone in soccer knows it. So how come, given the local soccer enmity between The Brothers and The Sons – enmity that's legend in Galilee – he's now hoping for The Sons' success? My heart is all with Nazareth. But in the present circumstances, since we're still in the second division, I feel I can spare The Sons a little corner of my heart. But, were we to gain promotion so that we play them again next season, my whole heart would go back to The Brothers – it would have to.

Say what you want this afternoon, Brother, plenty of hearts are beating fast for Sakhnin. The game fluctuates: 0-1, 2-1, 2-3, and finally – literally in the last four minutes – another turnaround. The game's changing heartbeat echoes in the tempo of the three powerful *darbukas* of the Gumbul Trio. In his stylish three-quarter cut jeans, bare chest, classic sunshades, cigarette in a Sinatra drawl, the lead drummer knows he cuts the image of any suave young guy at a Tel Aviv beach after-party. He insists on a distinction: No Hebrew, no English, only Arabic here. At first, the game controls Gumbul. When Sakhnin trail, his beat is solemn, a funeral march. When his Sons are dominant, his beat is a pillar of support. At 2–3 down, Sakhnin sink into the doldrums. The *darbukas* fall silent. Then, the crescendo finish: in injury time, Gumbul takes control of the game, lead drummer immersed in a mission. The Sons match his beat. They score twice – 1–2; 4–3. final whistle. Final score: Sakhnin 4, Beersheba 3.

Yalla, Sakhnin, *yalla*.

He who has not seen the Chairman's face when Sakhnin

equalise for the second time knows not the meaning of relief. He who has not seen Mazen's face when Sakhnin score the winning goal knows not the meaning of joy. No Hebrew, Gumbul? At the final whistle, the chant is the same as at any successful ground – *Adom oleh*! Red is rising! *Adom oleh*! *Adom oleh*! Gumbul is carried away by the Hebrew tune, carries the Hebrew tune himself.

This season, every game is a Cup Final.

UEFA Cup 2nd leg – FK Partizani Tirane v Bnei Sakhnin

There was a spot of déjà vu on the Balkan Airline charter that ferried The Sons into Tirana (circuitously, via Varna in Bulgaria). On board, the flight attendant goes through the motions of the safety routine demonstration. Abbas applauds her efforts. The captain's a good cheerleader. Those not already asleep follow suit. Diligently, Abbas fastens his seatbelt: Maybe you can you lend us a couple of those yellow life jackets – we may need them to survive the day after tomorrow? I don't even know where Albania is. It's only a diversion. We know that our real game is at home. If we can survive our league, then we can say we've won. This is just a business trip, come and go.

Veni, vidi, vici.

It's sunset as the plane takes off. Spot-on for prayer time – but I'll wait until the 'Fasten Seatbelts' sign is switched off. But the sign remains switched on – there's unexpected turbulence. Abbas doesn't like being kept in check. He's the kind of player who likes to roam the pitch, find the openings. I'm the captain. I take orders from no one but Lachman. When a game is going nowhere, Abbas is exactly the kind of midfielder you want, capable of turning things around. He adapts well to changing conditions. Unfazed, he stays in his seat, seatbelt firmly clasped. There'll be no kneeling in the narrow aisle this evening. In silent, otherwise motionless devotion, he turns his head left, then back to the centre, right, centre. Behind him, Avi Danan, the big central defender, is there as usual, as cover for his captain. I have the door covered, don't worry, we'll come out of this safely, we'll get back home. Strapped to his seat, his large body squeezed against the emergency exit, Avi bows back and forth, offering the Jewish prayer for a safe journey. Agoye responds: Amen! Go in peace, come back in peace. The plane is fast becoming an ecumenical temple, a flying temple of all faiths. In front of Abbas, Alain Ekakanga Massoudi, the live-wire Congolese-French playmaker, bowls over his left arm nearly colliding with the passing stewardess with the tray of flat drinks. Do you want a bit of a rubdown on that shoulder, Alain? Eid Yamin, the team masseur, extends an elastic arm around the side of the seat in front. His palm's already oiled at the ready. Across the aisle, Hilik Eliaz, the reserve goalie, always ready for a bit of friendly fun, pokes Alain on his sensitive arm. Hey, Alain, happy to be in Israel? Yes, yes, fine, fine. Another prod: You sure you like Israel? I like the girls in Israel, bugger off!

It's past midnight. A few stray dogs bark in the dark. Otherwise, all's dead quiet in Skanderberg Square. Facing Tirana's main mosque in one corner of the square, the central square of the Albanian capital, The Sons and supporters are checking into the Tirana International. A handful of debonair policemen cool their heels on the steps outside – hardly the kind of tight security Israeli teams abroad encounter these days. The players head for bed. A few disoriented fans are still trying to get their bearings. Albania is staunchly old Europe in the sense that religion is regarded as belonging to the private domain. Although 70 per cent Moslem, Islam here is stereotyped as a fanatical force – as some of the Sakhnin faithful are soon to discover. They ask the policemen for the *qibla*, the direction to Mecca. One points vaguely towards the south-east beyond the stark Balkan hills which dominate Tirana and which helped Albania seclude itself for half a century until, barely a dozen years ago, it finally discarded its communist doctrine. For the fans, the policemen are co-religionists after all. They embark on a strangely light-hearted, almost naïve, play of friendship, pretending to engage in the Moslem call of *'Allahu akbar'* – 'God is greatest' – they chant in unison. The show of religious fraternity goes only as far as it goes. Smiling but firm, one of the uniformed Albanians interrupts: *'Allahu akbar*, okay, but no kamikaze!' Religious fraternity, okay, but no Moslem Brotherhood. All Arabs are Arab, okay, but suicide bombers? It's a darn sight blunter than the unspoken things they hear back home. Sakhnin is fast realising that just about the only thing that all Albanian policemen know about their country and their 'historic mission' here is that they are from the Middle East, from a country that's the same size (minus the West Bank and Gaza) as their own. And, that they're part of a world with a renowned record of violence.

Something else bothers the faithful: how come their Albanian hosts show so little interest in Sakhnin? 'International soccer' may be a rather grandiose appellation for this encounter, but don't they recognise that, if not 'historic', this is a defining moment? In a country that's 20 per cent Christian, 10 per cent Atheist, alongside the Moslem majority, it matters little whether the visitors are Jews or Arabs. They are simply 'Israelis'– Jewish players, Arab club, who cares? That's underlined the next morning when Ne'eman Haleileh, one of the travelling fans, comes rushing into the International's lobby, all worked up with the news that a kiosk down the road is billing its tickets for the game as: 'Partizani versus Bnei Israel', literally 'Sons of Israel', or in its Biblical rendering, 'The Jews'. Ne'eman is put out by the disputable promotion: In Israel we're Arabs. In the Arab world, we're Israelis. Now suddenly, we're Jews?

An alternative billing for the match might be 'Little Sakhnin v Little Albania' – two societies on the fringe, each wrapped up in its own quest: Isolated Albania aspiring to acceptance in Europe, alienated Sakhnin aspiring to acceptance in Israel.

During Enver Hoxha's fanatical communist rule, all religion was strictly outlawed. Happily that's allowed soccer to become our national religion. Saleur Mulette, an Albanian league player, says that many, just like their visitors from Galilee, prefer to hoist the flag of the biggest world faith – international soccer. King Soccer overrules Sakhnin spokesman Ghazal's pre-match imagery of 'Third World meeting Third World in the First World', of 'Islam in Europe', exposing it as worn-out wisdom.

The ardours of life in Albania bring the 'Third World battle' analogy back into play. The state of the little main road leading into Tirana from the proudly named 'Nene (Mother) Tereza International Airport', named for their famed 'Nun of Calcutta', made its mark. When the team's coach left the airport it soon had to stop to allow an oncoming truck room to cross a bridge wide enough for just a single vehicle. These potholes make Sah Mahmoud feel right at home: Just like coming into Sakhnin from the town of Arabeh, eh Mazen? Sah, a Galilee representative on the Israeli FA, gives the Chairman a friendly pat on the shoulder. Sah is in the lobby, smoking the *nargileh* pipe which he's brought with him from Arabeh. He laments that Islam in Albania is something of an oxymoron: They're only Moslem in name. At the breakfast buffet, he scribbles warning notes to his friends which he attaches to the impious sliced-meat dishes, '*Hanazir – Haram*! Pork – Forbidden!' There's no room for pork on Israeli dishes, not in Jewish Israel nor in Arab Israel. Irreligious as most of the Jewish players in the team are, this is one issue on which they see absolutely eye to eye with the Moslems in the club.

FK Partizani Tirane, once the Albanian army club, has a proud soccer tradition. They've won 14 league titles and 14 cup competitions over the last 50 years. The club has 1,500 registered players of all ages in its various teams. No wonder that, amid the derelict communist-era tenements, kickabouts are under way on every vacant lot. Face it Sah, face it Ne'eman, Sakhnin are little more than a diversion. Albanian eyes are turned to the following week's World Cup qualifier against the champions of Europe, Greece. Despite the modest record of their national team, there's some confidence that Albania can beat their mighty neighbours. This goes against the grain of a self-effacing national ethos: Albanians still find it difficult to cast off their image as Europe's great underdogs – off the soccer field. Edgar is a soccer devotee. We Albanians are curiously unpredictable. We always come up with the unexpected, so when we expect to win, we always lose, and when we expect to lose, we win.

What does he expect next week? Edgar expects to lose. Hardly the Sakhnin mindset.

In Forsina Plaku, six games are going on simultaneously on a string of dusty fields. This run-down quarter of the Albanian capital is home of the Partisans. It's a shock for the visitors from Sakhnin to discover that they're not the world's only deprived club. The bumpy and water-strewn unpaved alleys resemble less the Arab towns of northern Israel, more parts of Shati, the Palestinian refugee camp on the edge of Gaza City. Sah inhales deeply on his pipe. He hasn't moved much from his vantage point behind his pipe in the lobby, but he writes Tirana off as 'just a big hole'. Ne'eman saw some nice scenery, though: This place actually has potential – anyway, it's darn better than an away game in Beersheba. The players don't see any of this, so they're in no position to make up their mind or to pronounce judgement. They're being well protected. They go through their training paces in the Qemal Stafa Combetar National Stadium in preparation for tomorrow's clash.

In a curious twist, The Sons have adopted something of the old blinkered Albania. Self-seclusion is put to positive use. Going out is off-bounds. They steel themselves within themselves. The choice is not to engage with the unique flavour of this country, not to tackle what it means to be a nation which has one out of every four of its citizens living abroad – Albania's biggest export, by a mile – though, as part of the Palestinian people, they share, like the Jewish people, the problem of how to cope with being a split nation.

The coaching staff sticks to its game plan: there's no need whatever for the players to go out into the streets. What would they see – poor gypsy children begging, lying on the pavement?

Should they progress to play Paris St. Germain in the next round, will the same restrictions apply to a café crème at Café de Flore on the Boulevard St. Germain?

It's all part of the Lachman credo to hang tough. Before

sending his men onto the pitch to play tough, Lachman needs his fitness coach Yoram Rosenberg to give the players the where-withal so that he can practise his philosophy: You can't stand up to the strong if you're not fit.

Like his commander, Rosenberg is fairly small in stature. He makes it up in forceful personality. The martinet sergeant-major insists on impeccable fitness. He imposes discipline not by wielding a little baton or twirling his moustache from the sidelines, but by leading endless warm-up runs around the pitch before every training session, even before games. Rosenberg acknowledges the problems of the 48-hour constraining order inside the hotel (apart from the one training session). Will they cope as a team? He's evasive: It's the chance to develop an inner strength by drawing strength from the team. Meet what Jewish Israelis regard as an essential ingredient in their national formation – *Gibush*, a 'Made in Israel' *esprit de corps*. A scent of army reserves is in the air – something alien to Arab Israelis who are generally exempt from army service – bonding built around self-discipline. A way for the mind to secure their target: victory. Shaping team spirit on good behaviour, it's called, the way tough-minded Israelis usually relate to straight-laced youngsters. They're kind of admired while kind of held in scorn at the same time. The Hebrew phrase is *yeled tov Yerushalyim*. It translates as 'Jerusalem goody-goody'. In marked contrast to the Hebrew media back home who depict them as a rough bunch of 'real nasties', Lachman and Rosenberg are creating a unit of 'Sakhnin goody-goodies'. Lachman, however, believes that a true goody-goody player needs to be a real nasty-nasty.

Put on your uniforms! Rosenberg commands his foot soldiers. No one balks. Throughout the 48-hour build-up to the game, no one dares take off his red-and-white uniform for a single second. Flip-flop sandals are the only exception allowed.

The one doubter who's not at all at home with this is Alain Massoudi, the Congolese–French player. Fresh from his stint with the leading Austrian club Sturm Graz, he has dismayed respect for the strict regime: You'll never believe how hard we have to train, far worse than in any other European club. They think we're going through bloody basic training. Three hours before we flew here to Albania we were hitting the training ground. We're made to crawl, to run up and down the Galilee hills. Carefully, he drops his voice: Our manager, he wants to reinvent soccer. The bonding, though, still has a way to go. At meals, a quiet confidence cuts across the hotel dining room turned mess-hall, but the tables remain mostly Arab, Jewish or African. Still, the meal is the same, the diet is uniform: no pork.

For all the seclusion, all the cotton wool, all the culinary sterility, soccer remains a risky business. At the start of the training session, Abbas aggravated a sensitive hamstring. He's out of the crucial game. However, his 'veni, vidi, vici' approach – striding in imperiously, speeding away winning, but without seeing – will survive him.

Inside the Combetar, even before the crowd in their home arena, the Partisans have given up any hope of besting The Sons. The Bulls are cowering in front of the Stallions. Even the most dedicated Partizani fan is writing off any chance of overturning the 0–3 deficit from the away match in Israel. Club officials too. The only one who can do that is 'The One': Gorg Teka, the club secretary, points with a single finger skywards. But, he lacks heart. God was obviously outlawed in Tirana for far too long. Anyway, it's too hot. So hot that after half-an-hour, the French ref calls for a short water break.

Sah Mahmoud can't believe his eyes: I've never seen that in Galilee or even on TV, not even in an under-12 game.

In the stands, there's a sterner contest, about winning hearts. Seven PLO people who are 'in exile' have ensconced themselves alongside the 60 Sakhnin fans from 'back home'. The seven, including a child and two teenagers, clutch two huge Palestinian flags, masts of a drifting ship. They parade their support for 'our oppressed brethren in our occupied land'. Sakhnin is their model for how a bi-national state of Jews and Arabs could work in one single state of 'Palestine'. Prior to 1947, before Israel, didn't Arabs and Jews play together in Palestine? We Palestinians are one family, one blood. Even though we live outside and they live inside, we'll fight to be one Palestinian team under this flag.

Up Palestine United!

Adi Gross from Lotem, a Jewish village over the hill from Sakhnin and a PT teacher for the girls at the Sakhnin teachers' seminary, is an ardent Sons' fan. Like Taysir, she never misses a game. She makes a tentative move across the bi-national pitch: Who are you? Where are you from? (Her Arabic is Hebrew-accented.) The PLO man isn't keen to give away much – just that he's 'a Palestinian refugee from Syria'. Adi's a little put out. She goes back to the Sakhnin camp, reports on her brief encounter: I like it that they've come to support us. But I fear that, back in Israel, that flag will hurt Sakhnin. The soccer public won't like it. It can hurt us being associated with the PLO flag. Ne'eman's good at diplomacy: Had Sakhnin invited them, I could understand that there might be a problem. But we didn't invite them. They came here on their own. And, who knows, maybe they're Albanians who support Palestine? Sakhnin shrugs off the brief encounter. They ignore the vain attempt at a political embrace, choosing to turn their backs on a mythology which they suspect is being woven around them.

Away on the presidium, high up in the stands, remote like Soviet-style commissars surveying a May Day parade, Mazen, Mundar and Ibrahim are oblivious to these pre-game proceedings. The flag affair is all soon forgotten, anyway. Political statements become passé when Lachman's steely approach begins to pay off. Pride in the unit – even grudging pride – stands Massoudi in good stead. His dynamism, his boundless energy (this isn't training, after all) are critical in giving The Sons a first-half edge which eventually seals a 3-1 victory. Out of frustration, on their way out, even the partisans of Partizani are chanting Sakhnin! Sakhnin!

Job done, Ibrahim exults: We came here to win – mission accomplished. We've made history, now we're going beyond history! Ne'eman's really getting good at getting things into perspective. Bollocks to history is the message on the coach back to Nene Teresa and (circuitously via Varna) back to Sakhnin (circuitously via Tel Aviv). The only mission is to win and to win some more.

The rest of the team heads back to the central task of handling the National League while Mazen and Ibrahim bounce directly back to Europe – to Monaco (circuitously via Nice) for the UEFA Cup first round draw. Ten hours after the jubilation of the final whistle in Tirana, back at Ben Gurion International airport, they've barely half-an-hour to rush from Arrivals to Departures to catch their follow-on flight. The reward of success in the Balkans throws up a daunting challenge. A mighty name is pulled out of the UEFA hat alongside that of The Sons – Newcastle United. The pride of the Sakhnin unit will face a stern test on Tyneside.

Chapter 3

Whose National Team?

Back home again

FORGET ABOUT WINNING. We can never beat Newcastle. Never, never – never in a zillion years. We know that – but we'll never tell our players that. We'll never let on to them that we know that. They need to keep believing that we believe in them, that we believe a miracle is possible.

The raw admission comes from behind the fresh tomatoes and cucumbers, a sentiment of all the stalls. The philosopher-in-residence in Sakhnin's open-air market is 'Sakhnin-Fan-No.1-Kfar-Manda'. The convoluted nickname is how Hilmi Bushnaq is introduced by Jamal Ghanaim, Hilmi's partner in their fruit and veggie stall. Jamal's Bnei Sakhnin's groundsman cum baggage-man who doubled up as quartermaster in Tirana.

Kfar Manda, Hilmi's village, lies 10 miles south-west of Sakhnin. 'Supporter-No.1-Kfar-Manda' comes across as a gruff

31

sort. From behind pyramids of aubergines, tangerines and bananas, Hilmi isn't all that keen to open up. You sense that he's almost regretting already having said so much. But you can't keep a good tomato and cucumber man quiet. And insist on a Bnei Sakhnin chat and Hilmi can't help himself – he's a sucker for a good natter with anyone about The Sons. Just like everyone in Sakhnin.

A heart of gold, Hilmi. But this particular morning, Hilmi is fuming, angrier than a grizzly with a sore head. Confirmed soccer nut sure but: I don't want any further discussion of our boys' so-called ill-reputed play – may all those ill-reputed commentators swallow their tongue and choke. It's just that it's distracting him from what's really set him on fire. Hilmi's wild because he spent a totally barren evening in front of a soccer-free TV last night. Frantically, he'd zapped his way across a galaxy of channels in the forlorn hope that some unexpected station would be carrying the World Cup qualifier, Israel versus France, which ended in a creditable draw in the Stade de France. It was a game all of Israel wanted to watch last night but were denied the opportunity to do so, Hilmi's Kfar Manda no exception.

The rest of the country is also seething – like Hilmi, wild at having being deprived of a rare moment's uplift. Last night, the national team was simply blanked out. All they could do was listen to the match against the mighty *Les Bleus* on radio. 'Shameful', 'National Disgrace' scream the tabloids this morning, angry that neither public television (Channel 1) nor the commercial channels, nor even the special sports channels had been prepared to fork out the necessary cash to make sure that the all-important World Cup game would be aired live. The failure to carry the game is the hot political story of the weekend. It's even threatening to cost a few TV executives their prettily paid jobs.

Whose National Team?

Like most of the country, Kfar Manda is served by Israeli cable and satellite networks. The game was nearly over when Hilmi belatedly awoke to the idea that he could easily have driven the 20 minutes across the hill to join Jamal watching the game on the comfort of his Sakhnin porch. Last night, Sakhnin cheered alone in the Israeli global living room. They've been soccerless for over a week: there's been no league soccer at all in Israel because of the two internationals on the trot – last night's game in Paris with another match coming up during the week against Cyprus.

What do you say about Sakhnin, quite something eh, success out of nothing, no? For once, someone in Sakhnin – in this case, Abu Ali, the owner of 'Abu Ali's', Sakhnin's premier hummus parlour – isn't talking about the success of The Sons. It's the TV coup that's got him gloating, the way Sakhnin managed to hijack the France game big time.

So this morning the whole town, Hilmi apart, is savouring Israel's goalless draw – as if they themselves had played an important part in the success. The rest of the country may be pleased about the result. Here in Sakhnin, they're treating it as a triumph. As 99.9 per cent of Israelis anguished, here the soccer-faithful (99.9 per cent of the town) smirked. Instead of being linked to the national cable grid, the 5,000 households of Sakhnin are catered to by a slightly dubious enterprise, the Neptune Network, an improvised pirate ship of worldwide channels and local programmes. As their jingle goes: Neptune links the town together, Neptune links the town to the global village.

Neptune's always on the ball when The Sons are playing. But last night they really delivered: they spotted and hauled down a special feed from a French satellite channel which was telecasting the game. The booty was another instance of Sakhnin self-reliance at its very best.

Sakhnin, 1; Rest of Israel, 0.

Market day is every Sunday and Wednesday in a dusty empty lot at the end of town near the site of the old-new stadium. Hilmi is beginning to melt just a little. When he was still fuming about his 'ill-fortune' in finishing 'soccerless' last night, he was literally throwing the plastic bags of weighed tomatoes curtly at his customers. The elderly woman shoppers were taken aback by the unusually rude way in which he barked out the price. But now that he's talked out his soccer frustrations, suddenly lots of 'thank yous' and other pleasantries are back at his stall – even an odd apple proffered to a child hanging on to a mother's long black skirt. Talking Sakhnin soccer is more than passion, though, as with any true passion, suffering is never far away: Put Newcastle aside. All I want is to be saved from relegation. Come next May, give me 10th place [in the 12-team league, the bottom two are relegated] and I'll be a happy man. That's my test of whether we'll have had a successful season – not how far we go in Europe.

Hilmi was not in Albania but he would have found a teammate, a kindred spirit in Edgar, the Albanian fan who'd found the perfect recipe for warding off ill-fortune for his team – talk of losing and be sure of winning. As a matter of fact, last night Albania also did well, - even better than Israel in fact – notching a dream 2-1 home win over Greece. For now, Edgar's fortune-telling hocus-pocus is confirmed.

Did Albania, really? Great! In Sakhnin, we're always for the underdogs, not that we don't also prefer the best. Hilmi doesn't want to give the wrong impression. Anyway, the tie against Newcastle is just two extra games. *Ponsella* is what they call it in

Zulu – a bonus. Precisely! Europe's a bonus, the league's the thing, and the second year in the league, that's always the hardest. Put aside our Cup win – we barely survived our first year. I'm telling you, our first priority this season is to survive.

Pride in Sakhnin soccer is everywhere. But underlying that pride is a wariness that after pride might very well come the fall. And, if you can overcome the fall, then the pride is even greater.

This preoccupation with survival, this angst about failing – it sounds awfully gut Jewish Israel. Survival, after all, is a national watchword. Something else, though. A role reversal: Hilmi's caution gives off the whiff of an old-flavoured Jewish belief in the power of playing oneself down. Before Israel came into their lives, Diaspora Jews, like other minorities, often felt they had to be protectively self-effacing. In certain ways, Arab Israelis sometimes adopt similar attitudes with respect to Israel's Jewish majority.

Hilmi weighs another bag of oranges. He wants to go on talking about The Sons' fortunes. But one of his customers is elsewhere. He's still focused on last night's game: I was impressed. I've never seen an Israel team play with as much determination, with as much courage – I take off my hat to them. It's the sentiment of the whole market. From his next-door pickles stall, Ahmad Tarabiya throws out a confession: Tell you the truth, I never felt too involved in what the national team was doing. But now that Bnei Sakhnin are up there with all the big clubs, and Abbas and Abed Rabbah are both in the national team squad, I feel somehow part of it. A bit of self-respect goes a long way: if Israel can 'beat' France, surely we can beat the English. Even if he hasn't come round to convincing himself, Hilmi wants his heroes to believe that they really can beat the mighty Magpies.

It's a stifling day. Unseasonably hot. Earlier this morning, the steep climb up into the Galilee hills had taken a toll. Past Kfar Manda, a few miles out from Sakhnin, the car begins to overheat. We stop to give it a breather at the entrance to one of the recently established Jewish villages that now dot this part of the Galilee landscape which used to be almost exclusively a mix of Arab towns and villages. The signpost points up the hill to Moreshet (Heritage), part of conflicting attachments to this land – a land where names become claims, where names replace names, where names re-enforce claims.

And – names calling names. And how! That's a guaranteed recipe for a rumpus. It happened again in the last league fixture against Hapoel Haifa whom The Sons had bested in the Cup Final and though promoted were now struggling to keep pace in the top league. It wasn't so much the sordid result, a 1-0 defeat, but what happened at half-time – all that positive energy from the final wasted in exasperation and anger because of a squabble with the Haifa security personnel. Some among the Sakhnin fans-turned-troops were incensed by a fast-spreading rumour that, during a minor fracas in the crowd alongside the pitch perimeter fence, one of the guards was heard to shout 'Death to Arabs!', an all-too-familiar rallying cry by hotheads in grounds around the country. During the altercation with the (Jewish) security men, one of the incensed Sakhnin supporters yells out 'Anti-Semite!' Let's say the anti-Semite-shouter was not literal, only sarcastic. Beating Newcastle in a few days time is going to be a piece of cake compared to trying to unravel the mixed-up mix of identities.

Waiting for the engine to cool, a large military truck draws up from behind us. The driver comes across to complicate identity matters even further. Sheepishly, he shows his delivery order for the materiel he's transporting and asks direction to the base. Gauging his accent and his disorientation in this maze, it's clear that he's *Russi* – a new immigrant from the former Soviet Union. His Hebrew is anything but fluent; he mispronounces the name of his destination. You continue down the hill towards Misgav, past the regional council there and the base is just before you get to Sakhnin.

Just past Misgav, as you enter Sakhnin from the west, the sprawling base spreads out on the hillside – behind barbed wire and rows of pine trees – rows of army jeeps and lorries lined up near squat, two- and three-storey buildings, and a string of prefabs. It looks like a logistics centre. The base has no formal name. Like bases dotted all around the country, the sign identifies it only by a long registration number – actually, the coordinate location on the 1:100,000 national grid. This – so reads the sign – is location 1003463.

Beyond the camp, onto Main Street and you're soon in scruffy downtown Sakhnin. Around the roundabout on Main Street – Route 805 – and up al-Aqsa Martyrs' Street, in virtually every shop window – from baker to butcher to candlestick maker – the rich red-and-white Sons' memorabilia. Competition is rife. Every shopkeeper wants to beat his next-door neighbour in a patriotic display of eternal devotion. Not just traditional soccer mementoes and posters of the glorious past but practical wares for immediate use: Sons' jerseys, Sons' T-shirts, Sons' hats, Sons' soccer balls, toy and real. The scarves have it, though. They're everywhere this sultry Sunday morn.

In Sakhnin's small Christian quarter, Haret el-Nasirah, crosses criss-cross the restricted horizon of the compact neighbourhood.

In one car, a real giveaway of just how soccer-besotted this town is: an amber-beaded cross encased in a miniature Sons' jersey hangs from the rear-view mirror. An icon to the best of Sakhnin worlds: a fusion of eternal devotion to The Sons with vows of eternal devotion.

Soccer heresy extends to the label that's proudly attached to the priest, Abuna (Father) Emile Ruhana. He lives in Usfiyeh village, 35 miles away on Mount Carmel. Every Sunday morning, promptly at ten-to-nine, Abuna Emile motors in to conduct Mass for his 800-strong Greek Catholic home-away-from-home congregation. He's referred to as 'our contract player'. Abuna Emile is happy to play on both fields: It's true, I'm a contract player. The bearded Abuna chuckles: Fine by me. I feel so much part of Sakhnin. Soccer's brought us all together. Everyone unites behind Sakhnin soccer. All Arab Israelis – wherever we live, Christians, Moslems, Druze – and also, believe it or not, quite a few Jews, back us. The team represents us all.

Everyone wants to be part of collective memory, a memory anchored in success. No one wants to be excluded. A season after gaining promotion, the State Cup is safely anchored in the town for another eight months 'at least'. A young congregant in his Sunday finery eases past: Hey Abuna, didn't you tell me that Mazen promised to let us have the Cup for a couple of hours this evening to get a picture with it here on the steps of the church?

Abuna Emile evades the tackle: Gosh, five past already! He rushes into the service. No chance to prod him further on his 'unified, all-embracing' ecumenical catechism. We're dying to quiz him on the fact that the tiny Christian community in the Holy Land is split between more than a dozen denominations who are sometimes literally at each other's throats. Is it possible that Bnei Sakhnin, the great contemporary unifying force, can do what his Holiness the Pope, the Archbishop of Canterbury and the Orthodox Patriarch of Constantinople have all failed to achieve during their visits to the Holy Land – elevate the Christians of the Holy Land beyond the millennium-old schisms and centuries-old rivalries between the different Churches? It'll have to wait for another sermon. Promises are exchanged for another Sunday when the soccer priest can linger to talk more about the condition of his 'minority-within-a-minority'.

Chapter 4

Goals to Newcastle

Newcastle, England

SEPTEMBER, EARLY INTO the new season, and an Arab club is marking the Jewish New Year. But there's a last-minute hitch with this evening's team selection: none of Bnei Sakhnin's Jewish players are keen to play in the key position. Fortunately, as always, you can rely on Mazen Ghanaim to come up with a solid fall-back plan. The club chairman sends on Kenny Brozin: *Yallah* Kenny, we're counting on you.

The Israeli restaurant-chain operator is definitely not playing his usual position this evening, but he's ready for the call. Deftly, Kenny takes a small skull cap out of his pocket, clips it neatly to his hair and, without any further warm-up, assumes centre-pitch between the cluster of round tables. Kenny clears his throat, opens a little leather-covered book and puts it on the dining table in front of him. Sakhnin's makeshift rabbi is ready to go. He pours out a small tumbler of ruby red wine. A tremor of interest.

The wingers move in closer to the centre circle. What's he up to, our reserve rabbi?

Kenny dips several slices of apple into a generous plate of thick amber honey. The ceremony is ready for kick-off. Rabbi Kenny intones the traditional *kiddush* blessing:

'Blessed art thou, O Lord our God,

King of the universe,

Who createst the fruit of the tree.

Amen.

May it be thy will, O Lord our God,

and God of our fathers,

To us, a good and sweet year.

Amen.'

Sensitively, he offers only a truncated version of the traditional New Year prayer more suited to the five-a-side game than a full-length prayer for the Big Match. He compensates for the brevity with warmth: A year as sweet as this honey – happy New Year to us all. The neat pass is taken wide-eyed by the team of Moslem players, Jewish players, African and Brazilian contract players, and Moslem and Christian officials. They're all exhorted to dip into the honey, to taste the 'sweet year', to join the chorus of Hebrew greetings – '*chag sameach*' (happy holiday) and '*shana tova*' (happy New Year).

Happy New Year, Bnei Sakhnin! Happy holiday, Sons of Sakhnin! May we, Galilee's premier soccer club, Israel's premier Arab soccer club, Israel's State Cup holders, go from strength to strength in the year ahead. This is Europe, my friends, we're here to do battle for the UEFA Cup. Next New Year, may we drink the blessed wine from that Cup!

Amen.

Mazen had arranged the symbolic service just before The Sons were to sit down to their evening meal. He slid it in just as forks were being raised. A modest ceremony, but a skilful tactic in this club of minorities – affirmative action at its very best: the club is usually part of the Arab minority in their homeland. This New Year's Eve, for once, they're the majority, a majority hosting their Jewish players who are themselves usually part of the Jewish majority in their homeland. This New Year's Eve, for once, they're the minority.

A substitute rabbi only, but Kenny (whose South African based fast-food company Nando's is sponsoring The Sons of Sakhnin) confesses he knows his prayers. He's deliberately chosen to elide over parts of the *kiddush* ceremony. The full prayer might have highlighted divisions between the Jews and the non-Jews in the squad. A definite touch of affirmative censorship, okay, but again, that serves our goal: to ensure that, just 48 hours before the key Newcastle game, all the club's minorities get on well together. This club are master dribblers. So many conflicting identities are in play, and yet, they seem to know how to avoid all pitfalls.

Everyone tucks into the apples and honey.

Kenny's not only a self-confessed censor. He's a self-made innovator, not afraid to tamper with holy matters so long as it serves the cause. His is a double cause – coexistence and victory, Sakhnin's cause. So he deliberately weaves in an extra blessing, his own homily. He tells the eclectic congregation-of-all-religions that the Jewish New Year is an occasion to be regaled with all sorts of special foods – not just the customary apples and honey; it's a time for fish, and a very special delicacy – fish heads. Our job is to make sure Newcastle become our tail, not our head.

Kenny's really getting into the spirit: Sakhnin doesn't intend to be swallowed up as Newcastle's minnows. Cheers of approval. The sermon's been a great confidence builder. Mazen smiles quietly at the success of his improvised New Year's Eve.

There's no fish on the menu, though. The festive repast is all standard fare, lots of carbohydrates – on explicit order of the team's (one-man) medical team Yoram Rosenberg – rice, pasta and a roasted quarter-chicken. Sit down guys, Bon appetite! Barks the fitness coach. Players and officials prepare to tuck into the real stuff. Forks are again raised. But Yoram's beaten the whistle. He's sent them off too early: Wait a minute, guys. Hang on a minute! Gather round again guys, make a circle, Mazen wants to say something. Again, forks are lowered. The club's revered chairman rests his hand on the apple-and-honey table. He speaks of 'our club'. Spare, immaculately groomed, Mazen speaks immaculate Hebrew. All the Arab players and officials speak good Hebrew. Only a few of the Jewish players know a smattering of Arabic. Hebrew is the lingua franca of this Arab club. The foreign contract players know neither Hebrew nor Arabic. All tuck in again to the apple slices dripping with honey. Stuck with the sticky apple-and-honey.

The Chairman's brief: *Chaverim* (friends), he opens. Unlike the didactic 'comrades' of the communist original, the word conveys a sense of real informal brotherhood. On occasions like this, families come together to wish each other well. We are all brothers. I want to wish our Jewish brothers a very happy New Year. And we wish ourselves all a season as sweet as honey, a happy season, a fruitful season, a successful season on all fields, and – almost a sad afterthought – a season of peace. He pats Kenny's 10-year-old boy gently on the head. All this symbolises what I always say about our Sons. We're much more than a club. We are family.

Adi Gross breaks into the traditional New Year song:

Shana tova (a good year)

To the whole family.

For most of Adi's Arab 'comrades' – players, officials, fans – the ceremony is a doubly revealing first, a first as hosts and a first as participants in a Jewish tradition. At home in Israel, that simply doesn't happen.

Several of the foreign players are dewy-eyed at this idyllic Arab-Jewish ecumenical encounter – even notorious tough guys on the field like the colossal but genial Nigerian, Edith Agoye Olomide, a believing Christian centre-forward. Even Abbas Suan, the club captain, a great practising Moslem midfielder, a non-sentimental sort, wipes a sleeve deftly across his face in the way he'd usually brush the sweat away on the pitch. Tomer Eliyahu, a non-practising Jewish central defender, a sentimental sort, disguises his feelings with a bout of usual neck stretching and ankle releases. Hilik Eliaz, a Jewish traditionalist and reserve goalie (cover to first choice soccer-is-my-religion keeper, Zimbabwean, Energy Murambadoro), covers all his (religious) bases. Mazen had taken Hilik by surprise, like he's taken everyone by surprise, with the nice ceremony. But Hilik isn't beaten so easily. He hasn't brought a proper head-cover for the prayer so he pops a pink paper serviette onto his head. It keeps falling off. He struggles to keep it on his head, leaving one hand laboriously covering the improvised head-cover. Let's hope Murambadoro's fit for St. James' Park. One-handed faith may not be enough to deal with the swirling crosses of Newcastle's Laurent Robert. Finally, Hilik gives in. He takes off his pink hat, takes the opportunity of the chorus of handshakes and embraces to ease the pins and needles in his hand.

Sit down, tuck in!

You're sure?

At last.

Eyal Lachman, The Sons' Jewish manager, a non-ecumenical sort, has been quietly watching Mazen and Kenny exchange their passes from his usual spot on the touchline: A year of peace, great, you're absolutely right about that, Mazen, we all want peace. But day after tomorrow, we fight the good fight, he wishes his chairman between traditional pecks on both cheeks. Lachman and Mazen, Mazen and Lachman – a bond of dedication. Peace and coexistence, coexistence and peace – the Sakhnin cheek-to-cheek gospel . . . but only if we win. Actually, peace and coexistence are a lesser imperative than success and excellence. And survival. That's their ultimate goal. Not much of a goal, you'd argue, but simply to survive another season in Israel's Premier League will count as success, as excellent success.

The way Mazen's accommodated the needs of their 'minority' answers a question that's been raised by Rob Hughes in this morning's *International Herald Tribune*: 'Has soccer become too big for its principles, must the game go on at all costs?' Hughes' column was challenging the decision by Europe's soccer authorities to compel the Israeli League champions, Maccabi Tel Aviv, to play a Champions League match tonight in Tel Aviv against Bayern Munich. Tonight of all nights – the Israeli champions were being forced to play on the holy day, a big family holiday. Here in Newcastle, Cup winners Sakhnin have indeed protected their minority well.

The Sons' soccer sheikh, Abdul Nasser Habiballah, is among

the several score supporters who've joined the pilgrimage to St. James' Park. The young imam runs a modest community mosque in el-Makr, a village not far to the west of Sakhnin: My first Jewish New Year – a real honour. He sees it as part of his duties as a fan – much more than as a cleric – to get as many of the Moslem players to join not only in the Jewish prayers but in the five daily Moslem prayers: There's no such thing as a non-believing Moslem, and anyway, it's important for our chances on the pitch. A cool sheikh – Sheikh Abdul Nasser Habiballah. He rejoices when even but one or two diehards join him in the religious practices in between the regular practice sessions. Drawing on injunctions in the Koran about how to treat the *dhimmi*, the religious minorities, he lives up to his surname, 'Beloved of God'. Habiballah, you're a sweet guy: Our concern for the well-being of the Jewish players is a quite normal thing. Looking after the religious interests of other groups goes way beyond respect. In Islam, it's an obligation.

Remember, as soon as you've finished eating – 10.30pm sharp, team meeting! Coach Rosenberg, ever the martinet, ever ready to give earthly and spiritual pleasures a shove – the sort of trainer who leaves nothing to the freedom of dreaming: And remember, no late nights. We've an important game day after tomorrow.

Of loyalties, devotion and the fighting spirit

And now for the apocryphal story of St James' Park. It's a packed house for a big Newcastle game. Only one empty seat stands alone in the 52,000-seater stadium. The questions are buzzing around Fred who's sitting next to the vacant seat:

Who's is that?

It's my wife's, Fred clarifies.

Where is she?

Dead.

Couldn't you have brought one of your friends instead?

They couldn't make it — they're all at the funeral.

Newcastle v Sakhnin — a draw in devotion. The only thing they know about Sakhnin in Newcastle is that they're Arab. The only thing they know about Newcastle in Sakhnin is that's it's a place where soccer loyalty is religious devotion. St James' Park — the Newcastle temple, a place unleashing passion and power, where conviction and loyalty are put to the test. Soccer demands total loyalty, denies dual loyalties.

Enter other devotions. Kenny Brozin, who conducted the New Year's Eve service yesterday evening, is having to improvise — again, this time as a sub runner. Mazen's dispatched him on a mission to the local Orthodox synagogue to organise kosher food. The synagogue is not a place where one expects to launch into an unholy football argument. But Pat Rotham, the experienced secretary, is on the phone to her chairman telling him about the Israelis in town. She listens attentively to Kenny's overtures. Pat expresses readiness to help, but is also overheard hoping this little club won't do a Hereford on us. Beg your pardon — do a Sakhnin on them.

'Doing a Hereford', it emerges from conversations around this football-daft city of 1.5 million, is code: 30-odd years ago, Hereford United, then amateurs from the Welsh border, knocked mighty Newcastle United out of the FA Cup. The collective trauma hasn't subsided. Soccer is a repository of long memories. For a century, the black-and-white stripes of Newcastle haven't altered. The city's Jewish community has faded from thousands in 1900 to just 700 today. But not their commitment: forever black-and-white. Not a single member of the community hopes, even in secret prayer, that the Israelis might win. They stand united behind their United. It's absolutely nothing to do with the fact that Sakhnin's not a 'Jewish' team. Many are genuinely moved by Jewish and Arab Sons united in Sakhnin. Sentiment hasn't shifted their support, heaven forbid, but some concede they're willing to consider 'edging towards hoping for an honourable draw'.

Games on the Sabbath aren't a problem either, but many of Newcastle's Jewish fans are disturbed by the New Year kick-off. The Jewish New Year lasts two days. So for all the purity of their dedication to the Magpies, however kosher it is, this is one game they won't watch – live and in public.

Avi Danan is also a central defender of Jewish tradition. He doesn't have any serious misgivings about playing on the festival. He really doesn't want to eat non-kosher, though. It goes against his religious upbringing. He's concerned it would offend his Orthodox religious family. Kenny's managed to convince the synagogue folk that, wherever their soccer loyalties lie, their first duty is to supply the kosher food. The standard kosher roasted quarter-chicken arrives from the Jewish community kitchen. All's set fair for St James' Park tomorrow evening.

To make sure, again the players aren't being allowed out, not even to grace the portals of the lone pizza parlour that sits between the range of outlet stores in the industrial park that sits across the road from the annex of the rather nondescript hotel on the far edge of Newcastle. They're certainly not going to be let loose to go shopping for bargains, even for new boots or Newcastle gear. Lachman and Rosenberg are demanding utter devotion. But what do you do when you're fed up with endless games of backgammon or hanging around goalless in Sons' training gear and flip-flop sandals in the lobby? You can always eavesdrop on your chairman holding court in the modest lounge. An endless string of reporters and TV crews are eager to fathom the mystery of the 'little club from Galilee'. Some still need to catch up on their sleep. The five-hour flight from Tel Aviv was followed by a six-hour coach drive though the middle of the night up to Tyneside – just outside Newcastle actually, at the Menzies Silverlink Park Hotel – then two more hours getting the rooms sorted out. Who sleeps with whom? Just when Ibrahim believed he'd disentangled any inappropriate couplings and had tucked everyone up safely by 4.30am, Mayor Abu Shadi was back at reception in his training gear and flip-flop sandals. He looks a bit put out. Ibrahim's called to summon up all his sharpest diplomatic skills: You realise what you've done, he chides the disarrayed young receptionist in a hushed voice, you've put him and his wife in a room with twin beds. He and his wife must have a double. He is the mayor, you know.

Mazen's marshalling his facts neatly: St James' Park capacity is double the entire population of Sakhnin. It's not their size that's significant, it's who we are, who do we represent? We want to represent Israel. The question is does Israel want us to represent it? If only it were that simple. Leaving Ben Gurion International, there'd been no ambiguity, so it seemed. There was a bevy of 'good lucks'. Ever since, Mazen hasn't stopped talking about his surprise and delight, especially that so many of the well-wishers were Orthodox Jews. At the ticket counter, one young woman stacked up a big 2-0 sign on a piece of cardboard. Many called out 'do us proud, represent us well.'

The question of who exactly is the 'us' that Sakhnin are meant to be representing resonates strongly with Israelis abroad – Arabs and Jews. A number have come to the hotel just to be here with The Sons, to soak up the 'Sakhnin experience'.

Over filter coffee and (Brozin-supplied) pretzels, Mazen lays out his 'I Believe' and what soccer can do to help. He talks with ardour: We make far too much of whose land it is. All we have to do is to accept one basic principle – that we're all here (in Israel, that is) together, and that the rights of all of us have to be addressed equally. Otherwise, he worries, our young fellows might tend to become extreme. In Mazen parlance, the 'our' leaves no ambiguity – it's Arabs and Jews alike.

The kind of 'young fellows' he talks of might well be two brothers, originally from Tira but now living in Sunderland, who've come to the hotel. They're welcomed with open arms and clearly feel at home. Kamel, the elder, has been here six years. He's studying to be a chemist. The younger, Hilal, joined him a couple of years ago. They seem firmly rooted in the north-east of England. Kamel sounds like a true Geordie: I confess I was never much of a soccer fan at home. But Sakhnin's victories – that's a thrill. He wants to be part of the success. They refer to The Sons as they refer to themselves – as Palestinian Arabs of Israel. A Jewish Israeli student, in England to master psychology, argues against the brothers: It's obvious who they represent, didn't they win the Israeli State Cup? Nonsense, counters Hilal: They don't represent Israel, they are playing for us, as Palestinians. He warms to the argument: Why is it that, only now that they are successful, the Jews want to adopt them for themselves? Why don't they always see us as part of them, even when we're just ordinary? He's prepared to take the whole Sakhnin identity kit – lock, stock and barrel: an Arab club with Jewish players, playing in the Israeli League. The Sakhnin formula – 'Sakhnin play for Sakhnin' – is good enough for him.

Despite the current mood in Europe vis-à-vis outsiders, especially if they're Moslem and Arab, there's absolutely no sign that Newcastle has any problems with these soccer 'others'. Quite the contrary. Determined by a sort of moral imperative to be the best of hosts, the Magpies inject a strong dose of affirmative action. Is that because their visitors are from a tiny impoverished club, such a minority club, or because they're Arabs? An optician who lives in small town near Newcastle has been drafted in to make Arabic announcements over the ground's PA system. He's from Nablus, the big Palestinian city on the West Bank. It seems Newcastle wanted a Palestinian voice, though he professes to knowing nothing about soccer. It shows: when the optician turned public announcer announces the teams in Arabic he gets the pronunciation of the Sakhnin names right. He's woefully off key, though, with the names of Newcastle's local and French stars.

Either way, as befits an optician, he's diligent about seeing things as clearly as possible. In the tunnel leading onto the pitch, he stops Lachman on his way out to his final training session. He wants coaching in the correct pronunciation of the manager's name and those of his Jewish players. Lachman obliges and uses the brief encounter for a learning session. The PAA says he goes back home to the West Bank regularly but it's become more and more of a hassle getting through Israel's military checkpoints: I was there just a couple of weeks ago and it took me over two hours just to get out of Nablus. Lachman, who's been listening sympathetically, asks one of the eavesdropping Israeli reporters, Where's Nablus? He's told Nablus' biblical name by which

Jewish Israelis know the Palestinian city: Oh, Shechem, now I get it.

Kenny's fish-head homily wasn't entirely out of the water. The extended roof over the stands behind the goals of St. James' Park looks every bit like a giant whale's mouth. Appropriately, he reminded everyone on New Years's Eve that Bnei Sakhnin don't intend to be swallowed up as Newcastle's minnows. He knows his Bible, it seems. During this holiday season, Jews recount the biblical tale of Jonah, saved by the whale because he puts his trust in God. Maybe Lachman will want to call Kenny into the dressing room before the game to drive home the story of the power of faith.

Al-Jazeera, the Qatar-based global TV channel, is here too. Estim Kritim, their reporter up from London, questions the Sakhnin players and officials over and over – you talk of coexistence, but how's that possible while there's war between Israel and the Palestinian people? The tone is sympathetic, but accusatory. At a news conference, Abbas glides elegantly through the minefield of politics and identities. His real minefield, Abbas confides later, was finding the right terminology in Arabic: You know what, I should've replied in Hebrew. I'm used to handling political questions in Hebrew.

The native British media have their own interests. After the news conference, the TV cameras are given '10 minutes' to film The Sons practising. Can you please point out who are the Jews and who are the Arabs, a stressed BBC North East reporter asks an Israeli colleague. For Chrissake, how in hell am I going to explain this complex story to my viewers in two minutes, and I've got a deadline in exactly one hour.

Praise the harbingers of harmony, they hail:

'In an age of overpaid, over-pampered and over-publicised players, it is hard to imagine football making a positive contribution to a burning political issue. But when Newcastle kick-off against Israel's Arab-owned club Bnei Sakhnin this evening the Magpies will be playing their part in a match which holds more significance than just a mere football match would suggest.'

Newcastle Journal

A romanticising of Sakhnin? You bet. The Brits are counting on their visitors to play *their* part, consigning them to a role so beloved by the English of foreigners – plucky underdogs.

How rude can an awakening be?

In his pre-match dressing room preparations, Lachman hadn't gone for the Bible. Instead, he reads his men an excerpt from a Churchill speech about how to deal with the 'Nazi jackboot'. No aspersions intended of the opponents, but the message is clear: be tough, even cruel, to achieve moral ends (moral ends for Lachman means Sakhnin's right to win). He warns: I don't want anyone holding back.

No one does. The Sons make a real scrap of it. Yellow cards fly like confetti at a mass wedding, and towards the end of the first half there are two who get sent for an early bath. It'd seemed at first like an inconsequential landing on the backside in the middle of the pitch. But suddenly Abbas is up like a taut spring, grabbing at the throat of the fiesty Magpie midfielder, Nicky Butt. They provoke a general melee. As they march off, the two miscreants nearly come to blows again. Again, they need to be parted by their fired-up teammates. Again, there's nearly a melee. Into the tunnel, again Abbas has to be shielded by his teammates from continuing to lunge at Butt. He's unrepentant: I never get angry on the field unless someone insults my family, my religion or my state. Who knows which of the three Butt violated. Abbas won't say. Echoes of Zinedine Zidane's reticence after his famous World Cup Final head-butt following Marco Materazzi's infamous World Cup Final taunt about *his* background. Usually, when a player is sent off for fighting, a manager is left tearing out his hair. This evening, Lachman's curly locks are quite safe – he doesn't say a word to Abbas.

There isn't anything particularly gallant or noble in The Sons' tackling. Their harshness has Newcastle coach Graeme Souness (no shrinking violet on the field himself) complaining: They came here with a recklessness to break the game up with tactics that went beyond football. I haven't seen anything like it in 36 years in football. Lachman agrees – he's taken the *Newcastle Journal* literally. As far as he's concerned this is no 'mere football match'. And, of Souness's accusations that he was 'beyond bounds' – you bet we were! Wake up: this is the Middle East – his wink and a nod riposte. Mandate-time Middle East, perhaps. Palestine British Mandate-time, perhaps – a time when Jews and Arabs in Palestine were, in a curious way, on the same side – at least in terms of their parallel battles to rid themselves, and their land, of the British colonial upstarts.

Lachman was determined to imbue his men with his own belief – not to lie down, not to play the gallant losers role assigned to them, not only in British sporting lore but by some at home as well. If his 'weak v strong' credo has taken the English soccer world by surprise, it's nothing compared to the shock which he's administering to the game at home. 'A blight on Israeli football', is how Yoram Arbel, Israel's most influential sports voice, defined Sakhnin during his TV commentary from St James' Park.

He wasn't referring to poor play, but to what's been designated by virtually the entire Israeli sports media community as 'Sakhnin's *sakinayim* (knifing) tactics'. Drawn from the ingrained image of the 'backstabbing Arab terrorist', it's a dirty play on words for dirty play.

This is getting into murky waters. Precisely, what's dirty? When goody-goody mainstream Jewish Israelis want people whom they accuse of being nasty to change and 'just play the goody-goodies', isn't that being dirty-dirty? It's certainly dirtier than Sakhnin being exhorted by their manager, a mainstream Jewish Israeli himself, a goody-goody incarnate, simply to stand up and fight a good fight back. And to win. Whatever the outcome of the match, goody-goody versus dirty-dirty, the people of Sakhnin look up to Lachman. Increasingly, he's seen as their saviour. Lachman himself is fully aware of the vicious debate that's swirling around his style of play. Sakhnin are being castigated. He takes a long and a sanguine view. He's emphatic: his hard-ball approach is constructive, and it's working. In Lachman's book, Sakhnin have already had a winning season simply because they've sparked massive interest, wherever they've been and whatever they've done; it's a great victory for this little town. Everybody now knows about us. People talk about Sakhnin all the time. Sometimes it's praise, mostly it's to attack. Often, they slander and badmouth us. But, just as often, they show they're afraid of us. And you know something – when people talk about you, when they analyse you, when they criticise you, when they attack you, even fear you – that means that you exist.

It isn't at all clear that Sakhnin is aware, or that Lachman himself is aware, that what he's espousing is very close to the philosophy of Ze'ev Jabotinsky, ideological mentor of the right-wing Betar movement and Zionist Revisionist leader of pre-State days. Jabotinsky argued that Jews must be prepared to stand up and take forceful pre-emptive defensive action against their enemies. A curious cast this Lachman, moulder of a pioneering Arab club for equal rights in much the same way as some of Israeli pioneer fathers moulded their 'motherland'. A goody-goody who believes that in soccer, goody-good is being a sissy. You could almost say Lachman's ideology is quintessential Betar ideology squared into a ball. It's going to be most interesting to see what happens when The Sons play Betar Jerusalem, the soccer offshoot of the political movement of the same name. In Israeli soccer, Betar are the traditional bearers of the fiery nationalist flame.

Oh, and The Sons lost 2-0 in the 'whale's mouth'. All in all, not a bad result.

So, during the long post-midnight drive back down the M1 from Newcastle to Heathrow (the club coffers didn't extend to an extra night in the industrial park), Lachman could afford to sound satisfied: Always think of the alternative. If that means being soft and gentle and a coward, if that's the way to get everyone's sympathy, then give me aggression. You don't survive by convincing anyone to like you.

A fortnight from now, de-romanticised Newcastle are definitely not going to take the second leg lightly.

Outside the National Stadium

The Sakhnin faithful face another two-hour drive, this time south to Tel Aviv for the return. For Sakhnin's Jewish neighbours, employers, customers, it's the end of the Jewish high holiday season. The holy season started with Sakhnin's game in St James' Park on New Year's Eve. Now, on Succoth, the Feast of Tabernacles, it's the close of the festive holiday season, the next leg of The Sons' European adventure. Tonight, they're the hosts – in the National Stadium.

A full five hours before kick-off, small groups from Sakhnin are already camping out in the empty parking lot. They're back in the Palace of Wonders, dreaming that there might yet be a magical re-enactment of that night when the Cup went up to Galilee. But this evening there's a trace of alienation. The village has come to town, but the town has turned its back. As is generally the case on Jewish holidays, Ramat Gan's a ghost town with the lazy Sunday afternoon ambience of any European city. Only a few eateries are open. For the Sakhnin fans, Succoth isn't really their holiday. Though, in fact, since many of them work for Jewish employers or work in Jewish towns, it's a long weekend. But it's certainly a feast, a soccer feast, a fiesta celebrating their inclusion in Europe, the right to strut the big stage.

When it comes down to it, the result of tonight's match doesn't really matter. Those who choose to dream can't actually bring themselves to believe in a dream result. The dream is simply to be playing Newcastle United.

Hussein Sawahna has brought his young son and daughter and, like many of his fellow fans, his own fare. The children tuck into cold drinks and snacks. For the adults there's an improvised barbecue. It all helps dream away the time until kick-off at 8.45pm. In Sakhnin you can't find a single soul who openly dares to admit he doesn't attend every single game. Were only a tenth of that true, Bnei Sakhnin would be a rich club on ticket sales alone! Tonight, the club has been very smart about ticket prices. Given the political tension in the region and the consequent downturn in the economy, it's a tough time for many families. Tickets on the popular side are priced at 40 shekels (around a fiver). In the main stand, they're 70 shekels. But there are discounted 'father and son' combinations, and special family tickets. There are lots of families. A mother wraps her little girl in a swathe of smiles and red–and–white scarves and flags. A smile to wow a Magpie.

Someone who doesn't take much note of ticket prices – he'll be at every game, wherever, whenever – is 'Supporter-No.1-Kfar-Manda' of the fruit and veg stall. Hilmi earns a wave from the group around the bubble pipe. He has a certain status, not least because he was one of the select few who made the hazardous pilgrimage all the way to Tyneside for the first leg. The man who waves to Hilmi from the improvised barbecue in the car park claims also a 'badge of honour' for undertaking the odyssey to Newcastle: I still can't get over that we lost by only two goals. Against the likes of Craig Bellamy and Patrick Kluivert, two-nil for me adds up to a victory. Like Mazen, what most impressed Supporter-No.1-Kfar-Manda and Badge-of-Honour-Newcastle was that send-off from Jewish Israelis 'to do us proud, represent us well'. They, too, felt it was genuine. From the 'enough-already-we've-heard-it-all-a-thousand-times-before' reactions of their friends, it's clear that, for the past two weeks since getting back from northern England, they haven't yet landed back from their shock and delight. For once, Jewish Israelis did themselves proud.

Those same nagging 'heard-it-a-thousand-times' questions

swirl through the apple-scented smoke that's enveloping the parking-lot–turned-parliament: Whom exactly do 'we represent'? Whom exactly are 'we' meant to be 'representing'? The same questions that taxed Israelis in the Diaspora – both Arabs and Jews united 'in exile' in Newcastle.

Lutfi Mashour, a native Galilean and a Christian, is a great instructor in cutting through defences built on dubious double loyalties. He's busy back in Nazareth putting to bed his weekly newspaper, *al-Sinara*. It'll be too late for Lutfi to get a full report of tonight's match into tomorrow's edition, but from what we heard from him a couple of days ago, Lutfi has got a good read on the result of the Big Match: Let's face it – we're not pure Palestinians, we're not pure Arabs either, and we're not purely Moslem. We say we are: First, Palestinians; second, Arabs; third, Israelis. But in reality, we behave first like Israelis, then like Arabs, and only then like Palestinians. We're Israeli – the way we think, the way we react, the way we eat, the way we speak. In essence, we're all the same, Jews, Arabs. We're part of each other.

Lutfi's a straight shooter. Salt of the earth. The kind of guy who's called in Hebrew 'salt of the land' (except, they mean 'the Jewish land'). What Lutfi says makes good sense: Not everyone's willing to confront their identity maze quite so openly. Many Arab Israelis would cringe at his analysis because it makes them seem like they've sold out on their identity, that they're kowtowing, that they're subject to what they themselves sometimes disparagingly call 'the *Mukhtar* mentality' – the state of mind of 'notables' from the '50s, appointed and cultivated by Israel's official authorities as a counterweight to Arab nationalists who questioned the very essence of the State of Israel, in short, 'the good Arabs', whom today most Arab Israelis despise. Many

Jews don't like his analysis either. For them, Israel *is* a Jewish state, no questions asked, a state for Jews. And, if you're not happy here, you can pack up; there are 21 Arab states ready waiting for you to solve your identity dilemmas.

Four hours to kick-off. Mahmoud Ghalia, journalist on *al-Ahli*, is luckier than Lutfi. The paper has already gone to press. So he can indulge himself. Mahmoud always likes to be four hours early: Ninety minutes aren't enough. I like to drink in my games deep and long, the smell of the grass, the excitement that begins slowly, steadily, to get a grip on you. You watch others getting into the right mood too, enjoying the hope, relishing the dream of winning – even enjoying the anxiety that, God forbid, we'll lose, enjoying the freedom, the freedom that comes with just being in the stands. If you come late they rush you in, the security takes your mind in a different direction, you lose that special experience of being trapped in by the game. Especially a game like tonight's game. How many times do we have the chance to play someone like Newcastle? I want to savour every single minute. That's why I'm so grateful to our boys. They've given us the freedom to stand tall, to choose who we are. Lutfi's got soccer all wrong. It's not all about identity. It's all about being accepted for who you are. And, we know who we are! We cheer who we are. We are from Sakhnin. We are Sakhnin. Take us or leave us.

Kick-off is three hours away. The parking-lot 'parliament' fluctuates between the last Newcastle game and Sakhnin's next league fixture. More like, is fixated on that next game after tonight's game. Betar awaits. Now that's a game that really threatens a major assault on who they are.

Betar Jerusalem – whose parent political party, the Likud, has been mostly at the country's helm for more than a quarter-century

– apart from brief interludes during the peace process. The Betar sports club has its origins in the youth movement of the same name which is uncompromisingly dedicated to the whole of *Eretz Yisrael,* the 'Biblical Land of Israel' as a Jewish homeland, to self-reliance and to aggressive self-defence. In soccer terms, the club has gone even further – it rigorously keeps Arabs out. An Arab player has never played, 'will never play', for Betar.

Betar lines up behind its symbol of the ancient Jewish seven-branched candelabra, the menorah – also a national symbol. Their colours are yellow and black. Whenever Betar is mentioned, Sakhnin fans see red, the club candelabra more like the devil's fork poked into their eyes.

It doesn't take much for 'parliament' to switch from the floor to the pitch, to the trauma of the insults which Betar fans had volleyed at them when they first played each other last season following Sakhnin's promotion. It hurt deeply when some Betar riff-raff yelled 'Death to Arabs'. Instinctively – it's not just outrage at racism – they hate the Betar fans for 'dirtying our common passion for soccer.' Armed with vivid memories, this is one match we must win – or, at least, not lose.

Felix, a Jewish supporter of Maccabi Netanya (Sakhnin's rivals last season; they went down to the second division while Sakhnin narrowly survived and escaped relegation) takes the floor. He too proclaims a love of the game. That makes everyone feel good again. The anger at Betar is soothed. Soccer is a unifying force once more. Felix has come with Tomer, his 11-year-old, to support The Sons. Why? Because with all my heart I'll support any team against outsiders: Jews or Arabs – it's immaterial. We have to win – no nonsense. Sakhnin represent the Arabs, Sakhnin represent Israel and, God willing, I as a Jew, want Sakhnin to win!

Yeah!

Several of the Sakhnin parking-lot 'legislators' reward Felix with hearty hugs. Yusef-fiery-fan-to-the-bone delivers a huge smack of a kiss on the cheek. With Tomer trailing proudly in tow, Felix's lifted high on Yusef's shoulders, a trophy of genuine coexistence. Even a tough-talking man called Tarek is so moved that he wanders around for several minutes repeating half to himself, half out loud: If only more Jews would talk like that.

Kick-off now but 90 minutes away. The gates will soon open.

Israel's Declaration of Independence states categorically that all citizens are equal. It also declares Israel to be the state for the Jewish people. In 60 years of statehood, the double-barrelled commitment – to equality and to national identity – lives uneasily. Is Felix's genuine declaration of support for any team which represents Israel – irrespective of whether they're a Jewish team or an Arab team, as he puts it – a pointer that Sakhnin's soccer success is prodding Jews and Arabs towards such national self-reckoning? Felix just wants Israel to win. He's still pretty much the exception. More often, fingers are pointed at Sakhnin, questions asked, demands made, that wouldn't be demanded of other Israeli clubs – that they be super sporting, that they constantly prove their loyalty, that they actively disprove the charge that they are simply masquerading, that they're pretending that they're part of Israeli soccer when actually all what they want is to play an Arab nationalist game. But such accusatory fingers are not here tonight. Another Jewish fan takes the floor. He's wearing black-and-white Newcastle stripes, though he comes from Jerusalem: I once studied in England and they became my team. I like Bnei Sakhnin too. We Israelis like our heroes strong. Every team plays to its strengths. Sakhnin's strength is its commitment. If that means playing rough and tough, so be it. Soccer is a virile game. They've been unfairly singled out, even demonised.

Demons and superstitions – inside the National Stadium

After St James' Park, Newcastle's manager Graeme Souness is a more worried man than Eyal Lachman.

When the Tynesiders touched down at Ben Gurion a couple of nights ago they were greeted by stickers proclaiming 'Israel Loves You'. Given the seven yellows and two reds a fortnight ago, at least Souness could take comfort that something had survived the six decades since the end of the British Mandate – the power of irony. Irony or reality, on the touchline shortly before kick-off, he's still recovering from the battering at St James' Park. He fumes. They played like they were possessed. He rants. But hadn't he himself described Bnei Sakhnin as 'the weakest team he'd ever seen in Europe – no better than a local works XI'? Surely he can appreciate that the underdog – a miniature underdog – needs something to give it a chance to compete with a mastiff. Bollocks, underdog be blowed, pure intimidation! They have a couple of skilful players, granted, but their manager's full of demons. All he wanted to do was to put the boot in – rest assured, that's not going to happen again tonight. Demons and superstitions. Kick-off is preceded by a brief ritual. Jamal Ghanaim, Hilmi's fruit and veg partner, sprinkles a 'secret' good-luck potion on the Sakhnin boots running out of the tunnel. Surreptitiously, he also sprinkles some of his potion on whichever Newcastle boots he can reach: It's powerful stuff – it works both ways – for Sakhnin and against Newcastle. Granted, Sakhnin had bruised Magpie pride a fortnight ago, but Newcastle graciously wait on the sidelines allowing the two Sakhnin bosses, Mazen and Abu Shadi, to be awarded 'coexistence shields', a tribute from Jewish–Arab groups.

Either Lachman has been singularly unsuccessful at firing up his men or the charms of coexistence are the antidote to Jamal's potions. Almost without bother, Souness's men prove that they're at least five levels too good. The Sons can't keep pace for more than the first 20 minutes. Alain Massoudi scores their only goal, an equaliser, but then nothing shields them from an avalanche. Newcastle demolish The Sons, 5-1 (7-1 on aggregate). Any lingering European dreams are extinguished. Still, there's a party spirit among the 15,000. They choose to enjoy the game as a spectacle, not so much as a contest. They cheer Newcastle as lustily as they laud their own heroes.

'Take some more tea,' the March Hare tells Alice, away in Wonderland.

'I've had nothing yet,' Alice replies in an offended tone, 'so I can't take more.'

'You mean you can't take less,' says the Hatter, 'it's very easy to take more than nothing.' For Sakhnin, 'more than nothing' has been playing in Europe. Freed from the shackles of the dream of continuing in Wonderland, the realisation is sinking in fast – Europe is not their real pitch, not the place where they want to belong. They re-engage at home.

Chapter 5

A Season Within a Season

From celebration to commemoration

PEOPLE OF SAKHNIN! People of Sakhnin! The Sakhnin municipality and the public committee invite you to take part in a major demonstration that will start in al-Aqsa Martyrs' Street at 3pm. Let the memory of the Martyrs of October 2000 be glorious and eternal!

It's Friday morning, the Moslem Sabbath – anyway a sleepy day. Perfect – the town has a hangover. From the European party, even though they lost. But there's no real sense of loss, or of failure, since defeat was at the hands of a European giant. No failure, but an abrupt switch from joy to pain. From celebration to commemoration, Sakhnin is awakening from the European dream.

Still, this is Sakhnin, 'gateway to soccer heaven'. Tumbling right out of Europe, Sakhnin plunges immediately into two defining events – rooted in memory and pain, but also in promise and hope: it's the anniversary of the killing by national police of 13 Arab Israelis in October 2000, two of them from Sakhnin, who were taking part in demonstrations in solidarity with the Palestinian Intifada uprising. Then, at the end of the long weekend, they have to host the old enemy, their favourite enemy – Betar Jerusalem. They're hoping their Sons will be able to reverse the mood – from sorrow back to joy, the joy of beating Betar. An emblematic mini-match, you could say, a season within a season.

Main Street, 10.30am. People of Sakhnin! People of Sakhnin! The public announcer drives his loudspeaker van up and down. Traffic light. No hassle for the van – actually just a small pick-up truck with a loudspeaker perched on the roof. Main Street doubles as national trunk road 805 that threads through the heart of Sakhnin and wends its way through central Galilee. But this is Friday and there's plenty of room, plenty of silence. The loudspeaker cuts easily through the rumble of an occasional truck. In the dusty side streets, the call resounds through the drowsy morning air.

Few people are about – apart from a group of 10-year-old junior Sons, already in their red-and-white jerseys, waiting on a corner under a fig tree to be picked up for their weekend match. An elderly man leans heavily on his walking stick. He heads away from the message blaring out from the loudspeaker, unfazed, doesn't even turn his white *keffiyeh* headscarf to see what's creating this awful din disturbing the repose of the day of rest. A few women peep out from behind curtains and from balconies. Most shopkeepers have obeyed the injunction to keep stores closed. A general strike has been declared this weekend in all Arab towns and villages to mark the memory of The Thirteen. Ranks, however, are split. In some of the bigger towns like

Nazareth and Shfar'am, the shopkeepers have balked. We've already paid too much, business is so poor we can't afford to close, to turn away our Jewish customers who come to us to do weekend shopping when Jewish towns are closed for the Sabbath. During the first two to three years of the Intifada uprising, alienation and deepening mistrust kept most Jews away from Arab towns. Suspicion still lingers. Jews are still giving Sakhnin a wide berth. Sakhnin has long been centre-pitch on the political map but wasn't making much headway with either the tourist or pilgrim trail. The tourist attractions are admittedly rather slight – but we do have our Sons. Objectively, that's something of a problem: without a ground even soccer followers don't have a shrine to visit. Shortly before the Intifada, they'd just begun to attract some weekend hunters out for a new kind of 'authentic' hummus, and to cater to the new fashion among Jewish Israeli tourists looking for something different, for a weekend in the countryside – an 'exotic zimmer' (as Galilee hostelries dub their B&Bs). Sakhnin hasn't yet made it onto the map of hummus. Today anyway, Jewish Israelis are unlikely to be here. It's a stage for recognition of Arab pain.

High noon. More people are out and about. Many head towards the town's five mosques for the main service of the week. Green-domed, al-Nur, Sakhnin's central mosque, is just a street back from the Main Street and Martyrs' Street junction. It's already packed. The *khatib* who delivers the sermon on this solemn day is Sheikh Ali Abu Raya. He's comparatively young, probably in his late 30s. Beneath the string of whirring ceiling fans, worshippers struggle to keep the midday heat at bay. Sheikh Abu Raya pulls few punches. He adds his call for a mass turn-out at this afternoon's rally. But the theme of his sermon is drawn less from the painful events of 2000, more from the searing problems of today in Gaza, where the Israeli army was locked in uncompromising battle with Palestinian militants.

Prayers complete, there's the traditional bustle for shoes on the steps outside the mosque. The call-to-prayer has been replaced by a different sound from across the street – the shrill clarion of a fishmonger, fresh with a catch from the Sea of Galilee 15 miles to the east. He hawks his attractions to the faithful: Fresh Buri, Denis, St. Peter's fish.

On the steps of al-Nur, between sock and shoe, a jolly reunion – with Sheikh Abdul Nasser Habiballah, the young imam who'd followed Sakhnin to Newcastle. He was our room-mate at the Menzies Silverlink Park. We track back a collective memory of that soccer pilgrimage. The confines of a compact hotel room are in no way the ideal floor for a prayer, particularly when two non-Moslem room-mates are taking up space too. Matching his soccer and religious convictions, between prayer times, the sheikh is an instant authority both on The Sons' preferred tactics (I used to play regularly myself in the Islamic League) and on prayer space (Don't worry, I can find my place, you be comfortable). Intrigued by the different prayer moves of different faiths, the soccer sheikh confesses he's never ever been to any full Jewish prayer service (or, even into a synagogue – no one's ever invited me). The little New Year's Eve impromptu get-together in Newcastle has whetted his appetite.

Out of his wallet he pulls an emblematic photo – here he is praying in the heart of the Newcastle goal like under an arc of triumph. Will he finally break his silence and reveal whether he had the temerity to include a special prayer for the outcome of the match? Sheikh Habiballah is steadfast. He smiles away the entreaties whether, on that balmy Newcastle evening, he deviated. If he did, the banter goes on, how come his prayer didn't reach its goal? We can't get any satisfaction. The sheikh is every bit as good as John Terry at heading away in-swingers.

The cemetery's no great repose for the dead. Perched right on Main Street, it's a raw place, even scruffier than the rest of town. A curious mix: a Soviet-style concrete monument dominates the graves of the two Sakhnin youths killed in October 2000. The memorial is bedecked with wreaths and bears the ecumenical inscription 'For the Deepening of Understanding Between the Two Peoples'. The sentiment seems out of place at a rally that's designed to be politically charged. An equally stark memorial to three other young Sakhnin men shot during land protests back in 1976 stands neglected among old graves, many of which, headstones fractured, lie untended amid weeds, brushwood and wild sage.

The through traffic never seems to cease, not even when the rally gets under way. A garlanded bridal car tries to dribble its way past the trucks and through the demonstrators. They traipse through the town, more a procession than a demonstration. 'Comrades, break the chains to freedom!' 'Forget coexistence, start with our own existence!' The memorial slides into political dissonance, much less of a political rainbow than a patchwork of contrasting colours – the red of the Communists, the orange of the Balad ('My Country') Pan-Arab nationalists, the green of the Islamists, the green-red-black of the PLO, plus a few odd colours of sundry breakaway factions. A melange of revolutionary icons – Yasser Arafat, Che Guevara and the clean young faces of The Thirteen printed on white T-shirts.

A group of teenagers wave vigorously a huge banner in the Palestinian colours: 'With our spirit! With our blood! We'll redeem you O Palestine!' An older politico tempers the spirit. Enough guys, enough! Watch the cameras, everybody's watching!

Not everyone's captivated by the old PLO call to armed struggle. There's Gumbul! Debonair on the metal pedestrian railings on the side of 805. No *darbuka* drum, but with his off-duty trademark – the nifty pair of shades – on his forehead. He waves gaily. Perhaps to a group of smartly turned-out girls, spick and span in their black-and-white Palestinian headscarfs? Gumbul follows his heart. Townsfolk watch in sympathy from the sidelines, women with their children-in-arms looking out of upstairs windows wave to the marchers, men smoking water pipes in the spring sunshine. They nod in solemn approval. Few get up to join in.

The march ends where it started – at the graveside. Speakers make the right noises but the run-of-the-mill dusty words offer no comfort for individual pain. The bereaved parents of Walid Abdel Moneim Abu Salah and Imad Farraj Ghanaim, the Sakhnin teenagers to whom the annual memorial is dedicated, gather in a little group, enmeshed in their own pain. The pain of the families is intimate, removed from the main body of the rally with its slogans and flags, as if excluded from the potpourri of political pledges and demands.

The purpose of the rally is diluted – neither support for private mourning, nor collective memory successfully channelled into political unity. How stark the contrast from the sense of unity, of solidarity, in the uniform soccer chants when the town rallies around the Bnei Sakhnin flag. In the face of victory and soccer excitement, political statements seem almost irrelevant. Does this have anything to do with the fact that the energetic lobbying for this afternoon's rally clearly hasn't worked? The turn-out from all the Galilee Arab communities adds up to barely a quarter of the 15,000 or so who travelled all the way to Ramat Gan last night.

Visible by their absence are Bnei Sakhnin people – officials, players, supporters. The next day, in neighbouring Kfar Manda there's a separate memorial for Ramez Bushnaq. This time, the club's heart is very much present. Hilmi is Ramez's younger brother. Their uncle Ibrahim, Bnei Sakhnin's foreign liaison man has made a special poster for the occasion. On his front door, over the photograph of The Thirteen, Ibrahim has nailed his motto. It purposefully carries memory in a very Jewish way. 'Everyone Has a Name,' the motto proclaims. The poster is in Hebrew only. Ibrahim says he's deliberately drawn the reference from Holocaust Memorial Day on which, every spring, Israel marks a solemn recall of the Six Million Jews annihilated by the Nazis. At the special Holocaust Day ceremony at the Knesset, members of parliament lead the reading of names of family members – name after name after name – recited dramatically by the first-among-equals and by ordinary Israelis alike.

The Holocaust inference is troubling. Ibrahim knows that, but insists: We make no actual comparison. We put out these stickers and pictures after that October. This sticker is aimed at my fellow Jewish citizens: 'Everyone has a name'. We remember that so many were killed in World War Two. But who were they? How many? Everyone had a name, a first name, a surname, he was dear to his family, parents, brothers. They are not simply numbers. People relate to the Six Million Jews as a number. But it's not only a number. Each one of them was a whole world. So, too, with us, it's not just 13 citizens killed. Each one of them was a whole world to his family and friends. Every one of them has a name. Remember as the Jews do, so that the Jews might remember you, is Ibrahim's goal. He's adamant. His uninhibited message is about recognising our pain, as he puts it, their separate pain. When anyone is killed, a whole world vanishes with him – a pointed reference to a Talmudic verse, a phrase much revered by Jews.

Ibrahim has a law degree, a masters in communications from Jerusalem's Hebrew University and was a candidate to enter the Israeli Foreign Ministry Cadet School: Thank God, in the end, I wasn't accepted – I don't think I could've pulled it off. Still, he went on to serve former Prime Minister Ehud Barak as Adviser for Arab Affairs. But the promotion to AAA didn't serve him well. Barak was at the helm when The Thirteen were killed after Ariel Sharon's controversial visit to Jerusalem's holiest site – the al-Aqsa/Temple Mount compound – sparked the Palestinian Intifada. Four months on, Barak's relegated and Sharon's promoted. He becomes Prime Minister. Ibrahim's a bereaved uncle: He asked me to stay on in my job – I couldn't. Twice, caught between a rock and hard place, whichever way you care to look at it.

Coexistence, reconciliation, reaching across, understanding the pain of the other – in this case, Jews understanding Arab pain. Hilmi's greeting a group of young men and women. One by one, they shake his hand solemnly, offering condolences. They are from Kibbutz Hanaton, just a mile away across the valley. Hilmi, with a five o'clock shadow of a beard, eyebrows that meet one another, looks almost menacing in his grief, permanently in mourning. But a most gentle soul, Hilmi – other than when he's roaring on his beloved Sons. He guides the young kibbutzniks past the phalanx of mourners gathered in the courtyard below. In the upstairs living room (from the stack of mattresses against the wall, it clearly doubles as bedroom), Hilmi chokes back tears. His visitors seat themselves in a circle on white plastic chairs, and listen: There were many emotional moments around my late brother Ramez. One of the hardest things to bear is the way people seemed to turn their backs on us. Immediately after Ramez was killed in October 2000, not a single one of our Jewish brothers came to offer condolences. Only much, much later did they begin to trickle in. But now you're here. Despite the situation when The Thirteen were killed, when you look where coexistence between Jews and Arabs is going, I take comfort in the fact that you can still find people willing to sacrifice for that goal. So I want to thank you for your visit. And I hope we'll keep on talking – however gloomy the situation. *Ahlan wa-sahlan bikum*, Welcome to you.

Ibrahim is soon testing the boundaries of coexistence: Coexistence – that's a phrase I have no use for. I don't need 'coexistence'. A horse and his rider is also 'coexistence': One rides, the other is ridden – perfect coexistence! What I want to see is 'us existing together'. I won't be ridden by someone who pretends he wants to live with me! He notes that the team shield has been very deliberately selected – the riderless Arab stallion riding a soccer ball, a statement of non-domination. A ride to freedom.

Both sides pick up Ibrahim's ball, proceed to talk about the Bnei Sakhnin model, of how Arabs and Jews play so well together under the same colours. Elad Bezaleli, the leader of the kibbutz group, says that a soccer match, though a small and simple thing, has amazing power to bring people together: We've got our extremists and you've got your extremists. Soccer can be a bridge between the two pains. Extremists here, extremists there – that's not really the kind of balance to ease pain – especially when everyone's united in believing that the other guy's extremists are a majority whereas their own extremists are just a small minority. Most Jews are convinced that a majority among the Arabs are 'just a bunch of extremists' while most Arabs are convinced that a majority among the Jews are 'just a bunch of extremists'. Soccer – now that's the real equalising force.

Many symbols died that October with the start of the Palestinian Intifada: for many Jewish Israelis – resentful and fearful of how Arab citizens of Israel identified with the Palestinian uprising – the idea of them serving as a bridge to peace died with those young Arab men who died here. So too, the olive branch.

The Sakhnin memorial march passed by a vast olive grove that spreads out like a silver grey sea towards the town of Arabeh. The original grove was uprooted in the '70s, the land confiscated to make way for a planned new military training zone, 'Zone 9'. Other land from Arab landowners had been intended for transfer to Jewish hands for the expansion of one of the new hamlets like Lotem, where Adi Gross lives. In the decades since, lots of 'Lotems' have sprouted all around the hills and valleys that overlook Sakhnin and the other Arab towns of Central Galilee. The Zone 9 takeover sparked major protests all around Galilee. That was March 1976, the original 'Land Day', another bloody landmark for Arab Israelis: six young Arabs were killed in the clashes. But, Land Day '76 also had an exceptional result: on appeal, the land was restored to Arabeh. Young trees replaced those that were originally uprooted. Asil Aasli was another of the 13 killed in October. When they protested back in '76, Asil's parents were about the same age as their son when he protested in October 2000. Umm Asil, his mother, embraces the twisted trunk. The tree upon which she hangs her tears is just about the age of her son when he died, a tree replanted after the return of the land to Arabeh. Asil had been an ardent believer in peace, an activist in 'Seeds of Peace', an organisation which tries to reconcile young Arabs and young Jews to each other's pain. If only Asil's tree could have been the seed of peace. Instead, it's where he was killed.

This is not only time for pain, for hanging onto tragic symbols and clichés. Even where lives were picked off, olives must be picked. The trees are real. Along with the loss, the trees spell joy, anticipation – of a season of get-togethers, family get-togethers, on the land. This weekend marks the beginning of another season – the start of the annual olive harvest.

Further into the valley lies a bright green patch, an emerald island in the silver sea, a balm for bitterness – the training ground. Soccer is now the potent force, the 'great hope' to redress a relationship without peace, without coexistence, without reconciliation – with pain. On the olive island, hewn out of a training field with a shed that doubles as a changing room, Lachman is marshalling his troops for the battle of the season, calling up his biggest guns: It's a war we cannot afford to lose, the war of liberation from Betar. Today, it's neither Churchill nor Ben-Gurion he mobilises to his side, but Napoleon. In the floodlights, for a moment, he looks exactly like the Emperor himself. He strides out to the centre of the pitch. One hand behind his back, the other tucked solemnly into his jersey, he builds his motivation talk around a pithy saying – 66 per cent of an army's strength is its spirit. I know that, unlike *Les Grognards*, Napoleon's grumblers, your spirit is 100 per cent ready for the battle. For all his largesse with big quotes, Lachman steels his troops by committing them collectively to his soccer ethos, a cult of simplicity: I know you're not spoiled. I know you'll be tough. I know you won't let me down.

From the sidelines, Mahmoud Ghalia is gathering last-minute impressions for his weekly column in *al-Ahli*. He observes closely the way Lachman prepares his team. Mahmoud's wary about his tactics: Sakhnin's soccer craze has gone beyond the touchlines. I swear, it's crossed all boundaries. Nobody takes any interest in anything but soccer. It's a sedative, the opium of our people. Sure, soccer often makes us feel a bit better, helps us forget our suffering. But then we awake to the same old reality. Soccer is trampling down our politics, even killing our politics. After March '76, we fell knowingly into a slumber, just got on with our own business – making a living, looking after ourselves. The Intifada woke us up. But, our soccer triumph has again made us fall back into political slumber. From the dreams of success, will we awake again to a brighter political horizon?

Soccer 4, Politics 1

Kiryat Eliezer is a neat little stadium, nestling at the foot of Mount Carmel in downtown Haifa. The Mediterranean is just a booted clearance away. Tonight, The Sons are 'at home' here. Given the animosity – let's not pull punches, the hatred –

between the two clubs, Kiryat Eliezer has the aura of a fortress. Mounted cops on every corner, batons drawn. No one's taking any chances there won't be a flare-up. The Betar fans and the Sakhnin fans are shepherded in opposite directions – they won't be allowed to meet. They take up opposing positions as befits their opposing positions on the national pitch. Separated by a whole pitch, even in the clear night air, chants and curses have a long way to travel to meet their mark.

Away in the distance, halfway up Mount Carmel, the Golden Dome of the Bahá'i World Centre, resplendently refurbished, shines down, though in the stadium there's not a whiff of anything approaching the glow of universal tolerance which the Bahai are pledged to sport. Soccer may pride itself on having a universal message but intolerance rules the stands. Haifa itself, once a major Arab city, still has a sizeable Arab population and likes to sport itself as a model of urbane coexistence. But tonight in Kiryat Eliezer, few internalise the merits of the 'soccer fights racism' campaign that's being promoted, with much fanfare, by the city and by the Israeli FA.

So what if direct exchange of invective is impractical. Each stand vents its fury, hoping perhaps that a sudden sea breeze will carry their choicest epithets across to the enemy ranks.

These are the Betar supporters:

Screw the Arabs!
Terrorists!
Collaborators!
Suicide bombers!
Hamas!

Super Shimon, the Superintendent, the Super Cop, has had enough. The Super storms into the crowd, chases after the curser and, over protests of fellow miscreants – let him be, we promise we'll keep him quiet – the irate copper hauls him down by the scruff of the neck and escorts him firmly out of the ground. One fan who certainly won't be playing any part in the excitement ahead.

I hate Nazareth, I hate Sakhnin, all Arabs out! Another favourite war cry, and two more Betar 'fans' who certainly won't be playing any part in the excitement ahead. By and large, though, the police seem quite happy with the level of excitement. Matters are under control. Just below where the Betar crowd has been parked, the tunnel leads off the pitch into the dressing rooms. At the entrance, some alert Betar fans divert themselves from the verbal assaults. They notice Mazen embracing Lior Asulin, his ex-star who had scored two goals for Sakhnin on Cup Final night and had then crossed over during the off-season to Betar. *Ahlan habibi* – how are you, mate? Best of luck, etc. Mazen – generous as always. Does he know something the Betar diehards don't? Will his affability be tested if his star ex-striker turns out to have a wonderful match? The Betar rallying cry is far less generous: Jerusalem, Jerusalem! Asulin Asulin! Betar! Damn Sakhnin! The embrace between their man and his former boss is disdainfully tossed off with an incongruous chant of *Allahu akhbar* (God is the greatest). In Betar vocabulary, in their minds, *Allahu akhbar* is the *cri de guerre* of the Palestinian suicide bomber blowing himself up – curse, not praise; threat, not embrace.

Someone among the Betar fans pounds away at a big bass drum. He makes an impressive noise. But the rhythms on his side are woefully short of those drummed out by Gumbul and his side-kicks. The Sakhnin trio is already immersed in their mission, whipping up the faithful. Yet, kick-off is still more than an hour off. The skull and crossbones banner unfurled beneath them adds to the menace of their beat. "Welcome to Hell!" it reads in English. They aren't about to be left behind.

Nasty chants are getting going on this side of the pitch as well:

Betar – all whores!
Rubbish!
War! War! War!

Right in the heart of the Sakhnin stand, someone burns a yellow-and-black-chequered Betar banner.

Betar's up in flames!
A small cheer goes up briefly.
Sakhnin's up in flames!

A red-and-white flag burns in the opposite stand: beacons of intolerance in a sea of supporters.

The teams are announced by the public announcer. Both crowds are exhorted: Behave decently (pretty please), respect the opposition (would you mind). Fat chance: Shaddup already, let us enjoy the game.

Betar chant: Death to Arabs, you bastards!
Sakhnin chant: Antisemite son-of-a-bitch!
Betar chant: Suicide bombers!
Sakhnin chant: Terrorists!

But Sakhnin have the edge in humour. They're less hateful somehow, though certainly ahead in noise. Hostility on this side of the stadium doesn't run quite as deep as on the Betar side. They greet their former star striker with the chant: Asulin you're red, red's your colour – come home. The player smiles through his warm-up paces with his new clubmates. Even *in absentia*, he remains one of Sakhnin's most popular Jewish Sons, especially after his Cup Final hat-trick. They regret his departure much more than they resent his joining Betar. There's a bit of a taunt in this embrace, psychological warfare, a smart way of putting Asulin off his stride, making him unsure where his loyalties ought really to lie. Perhaps the pro-Asulin sentiment is genuine. Or maybe they just like the guy, like Abbas speaking from his heart: We never forget anyone who gives his soul for the club. You never abandon a Son. In our book, Asulin will always be okay. For The Sons, commitment is paramount: once a Son of Sakhnin, always a Son of Sakhnin, on the scale of the lead chant of the Israeli army's elite paras – once a paratrooper, always a paratrooper.

For all the noise, for all the bravado, Sakhnin are subdued. Collectively, individually, they've been preparing themselves not only for glory – they don't want the worst to creep up on them, unexpectedly. But, unlike in Europe, there's simply no contemplating defeat. Give us a tiny one-nil – even a draw, whisper those without any self-confidence – and we'll go home satisfied. Even the most fervent allow this as the pre-match mantra. It's all part of Hilmi's constant fall-back position – how to survive in the top league.

Two minutes after the opening whistle, a whole new mindset. Sakhnin score. No longer survival, but glory. Confetti rains down, pandemonium. Until this evening Kleber Rodriguez, the Brazilian striker, has huffed and puffed, fumbled and fluffed. But he too understands the occasion. Finally, he's on the scoresheet. Celebrations for Kleber's goal have hardly begun in earnest when another cross from the right gets the Betar defence into the muddle of all muddles; their fullback gets his knickers in a twist, and the second goes in off the boot of Betar's Nigerian defender. You ape, you! – from the Betar stands. I love that guy – from the Sakhnin side. Own goal, who cares? It's 2-0. Heaven's touched down.

This is too much like a dream. Will anyone awake to reality? Soccer watching? Who cares – only the impure, the purists who think soccer's just soccer. Too busy dancing and celebrating. A trance party with Gumbul as MC: his beat reaches a new lofty pitch. The Beduin Boys Quartet have come all the way up from the southern town of Rahat. You wouldn't have known they've made a 160-mile journey up from the Negev desert. Black, gold-embroidered veiling robes (*abaya*) shine brightly in the floodlights, *keffiyeh* headdresses bounce in time with the Gumbul beat. Will their dancing ever stop? If it stays this way, the 160 miles back will be a breeze, pure joy.

The revellers are in no condition to cope with what's to come. On 18 minutes, they're dreaming again. Abbas slams in a shot from 30 yards. Unstoppable, Sakhnin's unstoppable. A few minutes later, Kleber pops in his second. Unbelievable, Sakhnin's unbelievable. Hallelujah! *Zagruta! Allahu akbar!* resounds back off the Carmel. The golden glow now shines outward from inside the stadium. The golden Bahá'i dome up on the hillside is a pale shadow in comparison. On the half-time whistle, Sakhnin almost get their fifth. Only an extra coat of paint on the crossbar keeps it out, preventing The Sons from notching up literally a handful of goals, all within the first 45. The 'nearly' doesn't inhibit

Ibrahim from signalling wildly down from his place high in the VIP stand with a full hand, five fingers, the sign of *hamsa* – the good omen.

Half-time for a necessary breather. The faithful dance on, ignoring the fact that the players have gone off for their break. They don't ever want the ecstasy to end, they don't need even a drink of water to rouse their spirits, they can't afford the time for the half-time toilet ritual. They're superhuman, transported into another world. Hilmi's as red as his ripest tomato, wears a smile as broad as his broadest bean and is sweating profusely. It's the heat of the game. Avram! He calls out to the VIP stand. Hey, how do you know Avram Grant? I know Lachman, Grant's a friend of his.

Hilmi wants to have Jews share his triumphant moment with him, not only to be with him when he's battered. So, why not Avram, the manager of the national team himself? One of the kibbutzniks who was at Hilmi's for the memorial for his brother Ramez, calls across to him from a neighbouring stand, at first a little gingerly, for fear that she might create the wrong impression among Hilmi's friends. She overcomes her reticence. She was so moved when Hilmi spoke about how Jewish friends didn't reach out to him after his brother's death, she didn't want him to think he'd be alone again: I needed him to know we're with him, this time in his joy. Hilmi has no inhibitions. He comes across to receive her congratulations, apologises for his soaked T-shirt: I had to come direct from work.

Soon, he must rush back to his post to live the second-half with his men on the pitch. Forty-five minutes later, his nails are testament – this is anything but a repeat of the first 45. Actually, they're almost the same – except in reverse.

Shell-shocked from the first half, in the dressing room, Betar must have been read their own special riot act – about national pride, about the disaster of taking such a pasting at the hands of 'Arabs'. They've ditched their regular goalie and replaced him with their second-string man. Altogether, they look a different team. Now The Sons are on the back foot. Within five minutes Betar have pulled one back. For 20 minutes, there's only one team on the field. It isn't Sakhnin. But for several muffed easy-scoring chances, but for that same extra bit of paint on the goalpost, this time denying Betar, the score could easily be 4-4 – be fair, even 5-4 or 6-4 to Betar.

Hilmi's agonising is almost too much to bear, almost too much to watch him bearing. Mazen as well. The chairman's cheeks puff anxiously in tune with the deflated drums of the Gumbul trio, a Red Sea puffer fish ready to explode. The four goals were enough to give him four heart attacks – only the congratulations fielded from all sides with every goal kept him from collapsing into a nervous wreck. Now, Mazen's unreal dream is turning into a living nightmare: Betar come close, close, and close yet again. But never more than close.

A collective calm settles back among the players, just as collective mania continues to engulf the crowd. When the final whistle eventually blows, still no one would have dared predict this result: victory by four goals to one, a soccer celebration that wanted revenge on the painful political memories. The heroes come to acclaim their congregation in the stands, and to be acclaimed by them, embraced by them. Hilmi can barely consume his passion. No one perspires quite so eloquently: When our players phoned me yesterday to say they couldn't come to the memorial for Ramez, I entreated them – don't worry, just beat Betar, those Arab haters, that racist club! Smash this bunch of racists, crush them – give me that gift on the anniversary of the killing of my brother.

Tomorrow, I know I'll crash land on reality. But right now, I'm on top of the world.

Chapter 6

Hosting Them at Home

'Us' v 'Them' – the oldest game

'We Arabs want to be part of Israel. In, not outsiders, not on the sidelines.

Our soccer is a cry, a cry that we want to be "in", not red-carded by Israel, not offside in Israel.'

Ghazal Abu Raya

MOST JEWISH ISRAELIS, including officials – especially officials in the VIP stand – believe they know the score with the Arabs. But their score doesn't include Ghazal Abu Raya's score about Arab Israelis wanting to be an indelible part of Israel. They go on chanting their score: We know what's really cooking in 'the *Migzar*' – 'the Sector', the shorthand term used by Jews to describe the Arab Israeli world.

Ghazal is not only the mayor's spokesman. He doubles up in many positions and has just as many titles. Ghazal's simply the biggest fan on the coexistence pitch. Throughout the season, he meets with as many groups from the Jewish 'sector' as he possibly can. Not just Jewish Israelis, also Jews from around the world who've been attracted by the aura of Sakhnin. His single-seasoned message is: We need to meet each other more and more, again and again, to create overlapping circles of common interests. Attitudes are slow to change. But Ghazal's a Sisyphean: he works endlessly for coexistence. He also administers the Sakhnin branch of the Givat Haviva Centre for Arab-Jewish Coexistence.

Today, he hosts a mixed team of liberal kibbutzniks and teachers from a religious seminary. We never really knew the Arab world, Ghazal tells his guests. The first time we encountered the Arab world was in 1977 when [Egyptian President] Anwar Sadat came to Jerusalem to make peace. My first landscape is the Jewish-Israeli landscape. Just as you didn't choose to be Jewish, I didn't choose to be Arab. But I am an Arab. And, I am an Israeli. However, my *Israeliness* is not mechanical. It's dynamic. Growing up, I never used to identify with Israel's national soccer team or with Maccabi Tel Aviv [the European basketball champions]. But today, my son Iyyad – he's 18 – he identifies totally with Maccabi. You ask, what's my identity? I'm Arab, I'm Israeli, I'm Palestinian. You ask, with whom do I identify? I was born an Arab just like you were born Jews. Yet, to the Arabs, we're not Arab enough and to Jewish Israelis, we're not Israeli enough. That leaves our identity damaged, crippled, incomplete. It's not easy when your state is at war with your people, and when your people are at war with your state. It means having to walk a very thin line, always.

It's not about how we relate to you, interjects one of his liberal guests, but what you do. At the start of the Intifada, we got all those riots. And you come and say: you're walking a thin line? Sure, it's a thin line! It's the riots that create the thin line, the nagging suspicions about you!

Personally, says the man sitting alongside him, I'm not afraid. I feel no need to be afraid. But I'm asking myself: Can it happen again? Will it happen again?

Ghazal is listening attentively, patiently absorbing the blow, his eyes already on the look-out for a convincing answer: If only Lachman were here, he'd tell them, 'When you feel insecure, fear is the best security.'

Finally he says: I don't rule out the power of fear. Fear may not be justified, but fear has its place. When you tell me: Ghazal, I'm your neighbour, I'm afraid – your fear may be misplaced, but I have to respect your fear. I can't tell you don't be afraid. Walking the thin line also means having to shake off those nagging suspicions about who we are, not just about what we do – behaving properly all the time, being tested for loyalty, day in and day out, like husband and wife – am I supposed to wake every morning with a song in my heart and ask my wife: Are you faithful? Does she ask me: Are you loyal to me? How many Arabs have been disloyal to the state? For 60 years, our loyalty has been impeccable.

Ghazal, I can appreciate all you say about us needing to understand you, says a religious teacher, but I sincerely don't see how it can work if you don't accept our goal, our vision – a Jewish state with a Jewish character. Do you fit into that? Can you fit into that? Look at what happens on Independence Day – we celebrate the creation of the state while you mourn your loss, your tragedy – you call it your catastrophe, your *Naqba*. How can you be part of the state if you mourn its creation? With all the best will in the world, you're living a contradiction.

My contradiction is your contradiction, says Ghazal – this time without drawing his inspiration from any of The Sons. You want Israel to be both Jewish and democratic, don't you? Then try to understand my contradiction. Perhaps it all starts from your reluctance to accept that we're here. Till now, the only way the country has ever paid us any attention was when we were 'disorderly news'. Now, at least, we have Bnei Sakhnin, and thanks to our soccer success, suddenly we've become 'orderly news'.

Thanks to The Sons, the 'getting-to-know-you' encounter ends, as they usually do, in Ghazal's favour, with a wishful-thinking compliment: If only all Arabs would talk like you.

Dreaming of a place to host a nation

Lavish stadiums the world over are the Mecca for fathers who want to translate their passion into the futures of their sons. How many dreams are played outside Wembley, the Nou Camp or Rio's Maracanã – fathers fantasising with infants-in-arms: Here my son is where you will find your fortune.

The stadium-in-the-building on the edge of the industrial zone has none of the pretence of those lofty locations. But it's on just such dreams that Nabil Halaj, a lawyer, nurtures his little boy. Twice a week, religiously, he comes here to keep an eye on the work to build the new stadium, the whole town marching towards the dream of having a new ground of their own. Jewish mothers are known to want their sons to become doctors or lawyers. Likewise, Arab fathers. But Sakhnin has loads of lawyers – several are on the transfer list looking out for an opening in other towns. No wonder the dream of every father for a good future for his kids is shifting. Nabil gives his counsel: My Asuna's only promising future is in football.

Asuna's not yet three. But, with a little coaching, he can name all the key Sons: Who's our captain? Shyly: Abbas. No need to say: Abbas who? There's a whole family of Suans, only one Abbas Suan – Sakhnin's prince. *Yallah, yallah, ya* Sakhnin, father and son sing softly in unison. Their refrain is choked by the hammer-hammer-hammer throb of a lone jackhammer, away on the old western grandstand, crunching the steps into grey rubble. The small stone wall which surrounds the old pitch is still intact. The sandy ground is still grassless. Still a long way to go. The prospects are neither lively nor overly promising. There's only the one jackhammer pounding away.

Abdullah Ghanaim – he's the jackhammer – has the same absolute dedication, hammer-hammer-hammering the concrete old stand step-by-step, stair-by-stair, to make way for the new stand. Sometime in the future, when, *Inshallah*, God Willing, Mayor Abu Shadi will finally come up with the necessary funds, Abdullah plans to rebuild it all. Dog work – what they call in Hebrew 'ant work'. Unlike a colony of industrious ants, Abdullah stands alone, a lone ant on the old stand. Painstakingly, he goes about his destructive building work, but he has no pain: Abdullah's working the Sakhnin dream. A singing ant with a singing hammer: Sakhnin *oleh, oleh,* Sakhnin up, up. The tall, willowy frame hums in harmony with the staccato of his grand piston. He bends low from morning till evening, both hands clutching the handle firmly in control of the pulsating hammer. He vibrates, he radiates: When they announced a couple of months ago that they'd finally be building our new stadium, I said to myself, 'that's for me, I must work on it. Whatever they want me to do, I'm game!' Now, here I am. If only I could sleep while working, and awake next season to find the ground finished!

Not so much asleep, as a-dreaming – a sleep-worker.

The moment The Sons were promoted a season ago, they knew that their compact old ground didn't even come close to meeting requirements in the top tier. A new stadium became the top priority. Funds, however, were scarce. Some money was promised by the state-run football pools, *Sportoto*, and as soon as Mazen held the State Cup triumphantly aloft, Ariel Sharon was on the phone, offering 'warmest prime ministerial congratulations', pledging financial support – 'whatever you need'. But the money's only been dribbling in. Much budget ground still needs to be covered: When will it be finished, *ya* Allah, when?

Sakhnin visionaries (for visionaries, read Sakhnin) parade their little stadium-to-be as 'A National Project' for coexistence, a symbol of national coexistence – 'for the benefit of the whole country'. Abdullah's very industrious. He's nearly terminated row 17. Only 21 more to go. Rubble's everywhere, tumbling all the way down to row 8. Abdullah's enveloped by dust. Already the place has the aura of a national pilgrimage. Among today's pilgrims picking their way across the clods of upturned earth, between the heavy tractors standing idle behind what will be one of the goals, are a group of 17 fourth-year architecture students plus their two tutors. Architects Yehoshua Gutman and Dan Hasson are conducting a workshop about the stadium. They're on a scouting mission from the Bezalel Academy of Arts in Jerusalem. Ghazal, the mayor's spokesman, is shepherding them. He shouts through the din of Abdullah's persistent drill: WE

HOPE IT WON'T JUST BE A MEMORIAL! A sad testament to frustrated hopes and ambitions. A bout of furious drilling from Abdullah drowns out what he hopes it will be.

The pilgrims from Jerusalem, as trained planners, have already designed their vision. They demonstrate the best of intentions. Gutman to Ghazal: You really ought to feel privileged. Everywhere else around the country, people are satiated. It's hard to drum up any enthusiasm. Hasson chimes in: You're the new generation of our founding fathers, blessed with the opportunity to be pioneers. Echoes of Lachman lauding his players for their simplicity, their passion to succeed, their motivation – they're the ones building this country.

Gutman is quick to set to rest any suspicion of architectural incorrectness: Jews oughtn't to plan for Arabs. Nor should we be talking about making a distinction between Arabs and Jews. Sakhnin is Israel, and Israelis can certainly build for Israelis. We don't want our students to think that their job is to reshape Sakhnin. He directs his caution not only to his students, but to himself.

Ghazal briefs them on the town's acute land shortage.

Then why not simply build high-rises, just like we do in our towns? Gutman draws the student into the correct mindset, reminding her gently that in Venice, the only quarter which was built vertically was the Jewish ghetto. That boosts his confidence. He warms to his role of 'helping' Sakhnin. Ghazal foresees the stadium not only as a place for 'home games' to be played at home, but also as a way to attract outsiders (like Gutman and his students) into town, a strategic device to break the ice about Arabs. Breaking row 18 now, Abdullah's hammer's in full voice: Hum-hum-hum. Gutman can't possibly hear what his host is saying, so he reads his mind. He takes Ghazal's dream a step further: The stadium will wake other Israelis to the fact that the attractions of an Arab town go way beyond hummus, pita bread and fava beans.

Once built, the professor muses, could the new stadium not fit into a reordered structuring of Israeli architectural geography? He's really humming now. Sakhnin will be part of a network of regional centres. The neighbouring Jewish town of Carmiel and the regional centre Misgav will serve as political and civic hubs. Sakhnin will be the sports hub. From just town to soccer city to sports city to . . . Still, the teacher-architect is tempted to go beyond his proclaimed 'hands-off' approach: Has any thought been given to the integration of the stadium into the community, that it should serve a grander purpose than mere soccer games?

'Mere soccer'? Am I hearing right? If only Abdullah would keep his damn racket down for a sec so that I can make sense of these guys' words. Before Ghazal can formulate Sakhnin's loud and clear response to the insult, Hasson, who until now has quietly watched the rubble heap steadily grow, throws in his two bits: Precisely! This stadium shouldn't just be for Saturday afternoons. It can play a pivotal role, trigger all kind of changes. Perhaps, it'll change the entire face of the community. He too is now in full flow. You'd imagine their inspiration will soon make the rubble bloom: This is a critical moment for Israel. It's so much more than politics – it's all about shaping our civic society – of Jews, of Arabs, and of what's between us. Yes indeed, I put great store in this little ground. Much could develop out of it.

Development's a process of change for the betterment of the community – Sakhnin's got no quarrel with that: How do I make myself clear above their condescending din? Whenever developers come here from outside, as usual, it's we who need to adapt – on their terms. However good their intentions, they can't help it, can they?

Before Ghazal can manage even a nod of polite approval, Gutman (or is it Hasson?) delivers the *coup de grâce*: There are several players on this pitch – Galilee, its shape, the infrastructure, the environment, the topography – all are players on this pitch. Sakhnin's just another of the players.

I must beg to differ: In this particular project, there's one and only one player and his name is Sakhnin Soccer.

Building their stadium is not about changing the face of Sakhnin, not about their lives changing but about getting what's due them now that they're in the National League.

Abdullah brings the issue down to earth with a bump, down to his rubble on row 18: True, we haven't anything, only soccer. Believe me, we love our soccer. Sahknin is not a soccer club, it's a soccer town. He motions to the spot on the old grandstand near where he's been working: That's our place over there. We've always stood there around Gumbul, all the way back to the bad old days in the Third Division.

'Up! Sakhnin, Up!

I'm red in my soul,

C'mon, Sakhnin, War!'

When will we finish our ground, when? When, for the umpteenth time? Abdullah comforts himself, invokes the Almighty in Hebrew: God Willing, in four or five months, it'll be ready for the whole country to come! (Hardly, if he continues to work on his own.) Then, we'll be able to welcome everyone as our guests, the whole country, even the Betar supporters – we want to welcome everyone here.

It's much more than stereotyped Arab hospitality. The buzz of 'coexistence stadium' is really how Abdullah foresees the new ground. That, finally somehow, once they have a place to host 'the rest of the country', finally somehow, the rest of the country might also just want to welcome Sakhnin into their 'homes' too. It goes way beyond just having somewhere to play.

Turn the other cheek v eye for an eye

In the olive grove training ground huge shells of discarded pumpkins lie strewn about. Through the hills Carmiel's tenements hover high, Arab villages dot the slopes, 'outposts' (the official term for the new Jewish communities in the area) clutch onto hilltops. The players are warming up for another lengthy training session. Overhead, a different kind of exercise is underway – four Apache combat helicopters manoeuvre in formation. The buzz of the choppers rebounds over Yoram Rosenberg barking out instructions. Who says power politics have been stilled by soccer? Who says coexistence has been redeemed by soccer?

Certainly not when again The Sons are caught up in confrontation, this time after the latest league game, a fiery clash in the southern port town of Ashdod. The violence erupts when Ashdod fans, led by Haim Revivo (until his recent retirement, Israel's national team star) when he burst onto the field following a sending-off of a second Ashdod man for dangerous play. He'd missed his high volley and slammed instead into Alain Massoudi's chest, leaving him prone on the turf, gasping for breath, literally in danger of his life. The medics rush on to treat Massoudi, but the Ashdod team management and fans choose to vent their anger on The Sons. The manager bears the brunt of the attack. They yell at Lachman: How can you defend the Arabs? How can you, a Jew, serve the Arabs? There's a nasty bite to the word 'serve' but there's an especially nasty bite in 'defend'. In the national psyche, it's the other way round — you 'defend' yourself against Arabs.

The fracas has the entire soccer community up in arms. And the political community. Within the corridors of the Knesset, concerned national leaders launch a political initiative and call for 'reconciliation'. The politicians are fearful that the sharp outbreak of tempers in Ashdod will shatter their vaunted national symbol of Jewish–Arab coexistence. A professional conciliatory voice suggests that the pastoral practice pitch would make an excellent place for a *sulha*, a ceremonial reconciliation in the purest of Arab traditions.

When news reaches the training ground that Mazen has agreed 'in principle' to play along and to embrace a *sulha*, dark clouds of dissent descend on the olive grove. Lachman instantly rules the *sulha* out of hand: Despicable — one day they're slandering you, trying to hurt you, the very next day they want to kiss and make up. Not over my team! What happened doesn't deserve a *sulha*. You can't be that hypocritical — kick someone in the balls and then do a quick about-turn and proclaim you really want to make peace! Those Ashdod guys don't deserve it. We can't possibly turn the other cheek. Not in my training manual! We were the ones under the hammer in Ashdod. We're the ones who have every right to complain about injustice.

Later, he quietly confides that he's playing tough so that no one among his Sons would even think of stooping to play 'cry baby'. That's definitely not good for us. Never complain. All it does is undermine the strength of the team. So it's not just not turning the other cheek — it's slap the other guy's cheek! Lachman insists the proper response to that controversial tackle should be a demand for an out-and-out Ashdod apology. So Israel's Parliament is left with an unusual stand-off: the Arab boss looking for compromise, his Jewish manager adamant that no cave-in should even be contemplated.

The fans won't let go: is this a case of 'naked racism'? Lachman's still smarting over the antipatriotic implications in that 'defender of Arabs' charge, but he refuses to face the dark spectre of racism head-on: In my bones, I can't believe it's that. He stubbornly refuses to call 'that' by name: As someone brought up as a true Zionist, on love of the homeland, on the good values of the Land of Israel, I just can't imagine anyone over there being motivated by that sort of hateful thing.

The fans keep on prodding: So what was the reason for Ashdod's outburst? Lachman offers a very prosaic reason, a soccer reason: Revivo's personal distress, his 'pitiful frustration' at no longer being a superstar on the pitch when he's now just a falling star off it. However warm their feelings for their manager, Lachman's euphemism is most unsatisfying to the fans. We've lived with racism long enough, as long as we've lived with soccer (as long as we've lived). We've had to endure it all through life in the lower leagues and now at the top as well. We're tired of it. How much can you take?

On the touchlines, the debate spills on over what to do — Mazen's *sulha* or Lachman's war cry? As befits a good spokesman, Mundar Haleileh rushes to take the heat out of the argument: Sometimes, the smart thing is not to react at all. Look how much

Mahatma Gandhi accomplished. Our highest goal is to be absorbed into the country as equals. The way to that goal is through the building of trust. I understand the offence but you don't build trust through frontal assault. You measure your achievement by counting your points in the league. Always remember, we're trying to do something different. We still demand our rights, but we want to convince them that it's in their interest to ensure that we get our rights. All around the country, people are watching closely how we react to provocation and there are endless provocations. No need for pessimism. It's a good day for those who like to both score their goals and save them, optimists and pessimists alike – as the Arab Israeli poet Emile Habibi calls them, the 'pessoptimists'.

Not everyone lines up with Mundar either. The fans may respect how Mazen holds himself back, but what they really prefer is Lachman's uncompromising toughness. They feel it was not only an attack on their Eyal personally, it was an attack on the entire club, on what Sakhnin symbolises: We're proud of Lachman's pride. He's a fighter, he's a tiger. And Mazen? He's real smart – let him play them in the Knesset.

So while they admire Lachman's self-abnegation, his readiness to sacrifice himself on the front lines for the town, his readiness to fight back, they also pay tribute to the contrasting public posture of their chairman. Half turn the other cheek, but slap back. Flip-flop fans, some might say. Anyway, a jolly neat two-step of tolerance and belligerency.

Journalist Mahmoud Ghalia, about to file his story, is wary of being as controversially, and as uncompromisingly, tough as Lachman. Perhaps what worries him most is the temptation to identify wholeheartedly with Lachman – look what Ashdod has done to us, me and Lachman in the same team! He looks edgily over his shoulder when he adds a blunt tinge to the debate – Don't quote me on this if you're publishing this tomorrow but it's okay for historical record: There are two levels to our battles. One is in democratic forums, in the Knesset and the like, what they call in Hebrew *derekh eretz* (model behaviour, respect). Our second front is the battle of the street. Lachman's the street fighter par excellence. It's a good thing he's here with us, heading our gang on the street.

Lachman would only partly concede to being the 'gangster' of the club. He's not here to crusade for lofty goals of equality and coexistence: I am devoid of politics. All I seek is justice on the pitch. 'Our street-thug' and a Jewish patriot in a tracksuit at the same time, he's cover for the team and their fans – Sakhnin's flack jacket, the great deflector of unwarranted attacks. A 'defender of Arabs', indeed!

What he defends is success, what he serves is victory. Remember what I always say, repeat after me: When people relate to Sakhnin, even when they hammer us, even when occasionally they fear us, that means they know we exist. Sure, Mazen's a man of peace, and that's good. What he does is very nice. Sometimes, when your cause is just, it's worth a two-footed tackle – conciliatory and tough at the same time.

Disconcerted murmurs in the stands: What's this – a new Lachman? Is he signing us on to the neat play of 'vigorous tolerance'?

Wherever they stand in this match – Mazen versus Lachman – the fans all tend to come back to one stark principle: *Ghas bin annak* in local Arabic lore. Liberally translated, it means 'We're here, like it or not.' Survival, existence, in the raw.

Existence is truly an existential matter here. Just managing to survive is the real thing. Existence touches everyone, Arab and Jew. Nobody takes it for granted. Nobody can afford to take it for granted. Everyone whose existence is threatened feels himself a minority.

Nonetheless, a *sulha* with Ashdod Sports Club has been decided upon. Mazen sets about agreeing the time and place of reconciliation. Hands have been outstretched. But they're yet to touch. Fact of the matter is, the soccer *sulha* is never going to take place. The league must go on. Soccer's paramount. With or without reconciliation, Sakhnin must host Ashdod in February.

Chapter 7

From Ramadan Through Christmas

At the Suans

ABBAS SUAN IS 28. Sun of The Sons. Like a '20s bright star, a Rudolph Valentino as The Son of a Sheik but without the sheikh's cloak and headdress, without brilliantine and eyeliner. Majestic. Earnest. Sometimes a smiler, though. No bombast whatsoever. Modest, naïve almost. During the holy month of Ramadan, he fasts: Always have – since I was five, Ramadan's another world. A month, but it feels like a year. It's great – you sit down together, the whole family, every evening around the table, breaking the fast. Now, as The Sons' captain, he feels a special responsibility. He sets an example. It's an obligation.

Soccer's-killing-politics-Mahmoud is in his office at *al-Ahli*. Abbas storms in. He's trying his best to show he's angry, ready to tear into the man whom he yells is nothing but a yellow scribbler: Call yourself a journalist? *Ma'ariv*, the Tel Aviv-based national paper to which Mahmoud contributes, has run an exposé that hammers Abbas for taking too literally the Lachman 'stand-up-tall-to-the-strong' philosophy. The article alleges that the captain caused a rumpus during practice by 'mowing down' one of his teammates with a particularly fierce tackle. Abbas remonstrates: How could you write such rubbish? You're just playing up the lies about us playing tough. Well, murmurs Mahmoud, half-way apologising, half-way defending himself – he's that kind of guy, full of strong views, but not all that confident, when push comes to shove, about pressing his opinion too firmly, especially in a town with a village mentality. He kind of expresses his regret: You know how these papers love to blow things up out of proportion. I assure you I never wrote it like that.

They're doing a sort of chase minuet around the desk of *al-Ahli*'s (absent) editor-in-chief, Ghazi Abu Raya. Abbas wags his finger vigorously at the errant scribe. But, though he knows he's in the right and has been the victim of minor-key sensationalism, he's not going to push his anger too far. When push comes to shove, he doesn't have it in him. Except in soccer – ask Nicky Butt.

They look up to Abbas in this town. Sakhnin likes to call itself 'conservative and tolerant'. Abbas to a tee. He's rooted in the town. No. 8, the number of his shirt, is the one seen most on the backs of little boys in the streets. He is their favourite Son.

The streets have a very distinct quality about them these days. There are few signs of anyone not fasting. Everyone works half a day. From four in the afternoon, the only action in town is in the confectionary shops. In Walid Hamza Bros., people are queuing to buy *katayef*, *knafeh*, *baklava* and other cakes to make the fast-breaking meal in an hour's time that much sweeter.

From Ramadan Through Christmas

No hardship, then, the fasting? As a player, it's very hard. Surely, though, a handicap in league games scheduled to be played during Ramadan? An unexpected revelation: on match days, Abbas and his Moslem teammates are 'exempted' from fasting. The whole town, even the religious fans, tell me that I should tell the players who fast that they shouldn't. 'We'll do the fasting on your behalf,' they tell us. 'Cos if, heaven forbid, we lose, a lot of people will lose faith in us and stop fasting themselves. We can't let them down. It's victory above all.' Abbas doesn't reveal if the substitute fasters either sought, or received, sanction from their Imam for their readiness to do a 'double fast' – for them and for The Sons.

Dusk. Five o'clock's fast approaching. In the modest front room of the Suan family home – a grey three-storey concrete house set slap on route 805 – the TV, marking the end of the day's fasting, echoes the prayers which blare out from the nearby New Mosque. Pots are coming to the boil. There's much bustle in the antechamber kitchen. Safa, Abbas's wife, leads the last-minute hustle to get the evening *Iftar* meal ready for the 'whistle' that will signal the end of the fast. Unlike in Jerusalem, the 'whistle' is not a cannon, just a programme change on the TV (tuned to *al-Arabiya* broadcasting from Saudi Arabia). Abbas takes a neat pass of dishes from Safa. He quickly sets them up on the 'table', a mat laid down in the centre of the living room, around which the whole family sits down together. Abbas, his eldest brother Ahmad, and their families array themselves on mattresses around the mat. Sa'id Hamad Suan, their elderly father, presides at the head of the mat. It's simple fare: chunks of roast quarter-chicken, rice and almonds, yoghurt – no frills, none of the traditional Ramadan sweets which we'd brought, thinking it appropriate for the holiday. No sweets please, my football diet, Abbas apologises with a shy smile. The town fasts for The Sons, but Abbas fasts anyway. A soccer player must set the standards for his home team as well. He keeps his family sugar-free.

Each of the adults recites a short silent prayer. *Al-Arabiya* switches from the solemn Moslem version of 'Prayer for the Day' to the rumbustious evening entertainment featuring non-decorous Arab pop dancing and noisy quiz shows. The family eat quickly, earnestly, even a touch frenetically. In silence. After a couple of mouthfuls Abbas's father turns to what he's missed most during the day-long fast, a deep drag on a fag, neat in a dainty cigarette holder. The meal over, Abbas and his father pray individually. Little Muhammad, 14-month-old scion of the favourite Son, continues to swing to and fro in his little light blue swing in rhythm with *al-Arabiya*.

On the wall of the sparsely furnished front room, the customary photo of the Golden Dome of the Rock which sits on Jerusalem's holiest site, the *Haram el Sharif*, the Noble Sanctuary (for Moslems), the Temple Mount (for Jews). Alongside, pinned with thumbtacks, a fairly crumpled old map of the country with a legend in Arabic. What catches the eye of anyone accustomed to reading maps of the country in Jewish Israeli homes or in Palestinian homes is the Green Line – called that simply because, on all maps, the border line designating the 1949 armistice line after Israel's War of Independence (for all Jews), the Great Catastrophe (for all Arabs), was always coloured green. In the 1967 Six Day War, when Israel conquered the West Bank – occupied West Bank (for the Arabs), liberated Land of Israel (for some of the Jews) – the Green Line was erased from Israeli maps. Here, in this Arab Israeli home, the Green Line has made a come back – a switch back to the time when Israel lived between 1949 and 1967 behind the Green Line border. The map shows clearly where Israel began and where Israel ended. That map is special. Every now and then, we look at it. It's Palestine in 1948. My dad was from somewhere else, not from Sakhnin, but from near Beit Shean. Abbas fingers his way around the map: Where is it? Here's Beit Shean . . .

Look for Nazareth, says dad from behind his fag.

Here's Nazareth . . . no it's further east. Oh, here it is. Abbas still has some difficulty locating it. Finally he puts his finger on it, stabs it home: I've found it. Murassass, a footnote from history near the present-day Israeli town of Beit Shean, south of the Sea of Galilee, near the Jordan River. Sa'id Hamad explains that the Suans came originally from Murassass and that during the 1948 war, 'we were pressured into leaving.' They relocated to Sakhnin.

Every year, on Israel's Independence Day that marks the outcome of that war, he and some of Abbas's older brothers make an annual pilgrimage – more statement of memory than forceful political declaration. Memory's a split matter, depending from which side of the map you come. In this country, memory's a serious matter, a state affair. Sa'id Hamad talks of 'the country going to the dogs'. He talks fondly of 'the old days' when Sakhnin was '90 per cent Mapai' [the precursor of the current Labour Party which ruled Israel unchallenged for its first 29 years, both behind and then, from '67, beyond the Green Line]: How could things have gone so astray? One day, dislocated Palestinian; the next, old-guard Israeli.

Abbas doesn't go on those back-to-roots family outings. Like many Israelis born after '67, 'the '40s and '50s don't work for me'. What he does – his soccer success – does the talking, not what he remembers. A propos soccer success, Ghazal always says it's already part of collective memory – 'a memory of victory', distinct from the memory of defeats.

In the modest home, there's curiously little indication of the trappings of Bnei Sakhnin, no memorabilia other than a postcard-size picture of the team Abbas led to capture the trophy and, in the master bedroom upstairs, a tatty newspaper clipping of a sleeping Abbas in bed, clutching the Cup.

By the way, where's the Cup actually? A family shrug.

The youngest of nine children (seven sons and two daughters), Abbas is the brightest star. Sa'id Hamad is proud that all the sons of his soccer family have played, at one level or another, for Sakhnin. This evening, the Beit Shean soccer ground is very much in his mind, not only a matter of the past. His son and The Sons will be hosting their next couple of home games there, including the much-anticipated game the night after tomorrow against table-topping Maccabi Haifa.

Father and son set out for evening prayers in the New Mosque just 50 yards down the road. Abbas, ever the pivot, has a clear conception of his place on any pitch. He strikes directly to the spot inside the mosque where he always prays. No dithering about in search of his particular row among the many rows of worshippers. The row opens up, other worshippers pleased to greet Abbas into their ranks: During Ramadan, you're duty-bound not to conceal anything which makes you happy. So, I must tell you, I am happy – a great family, and success in soccer. Only one dream remains unfulfilled – to be chosen to play in the Israeli national team and that we'll win through to the World Cup Finals.

Friendship

High-flying dreams are prayed – each dreamer to his own, each worshipper with the words singular to his religion, each in his own language and code of devotion. Common to all, a monotheistic dream, a prosaic faith: Just let us win tonight. Not so much an ecumenical meeting of the faithful as a cross-pollination of prayers: Abed Rabbah bows his head, hands clasped across his chest in silent prayer; Agoye Olomide crosses himself neatly, eloquently; Avi Danan brushes his fingertips to his lips after brushing the religious text on the doorpost leading out from the dressing room. In the tunnel leading onto the pitch, each is deep in his own brief prayer, the silence troubled only by the constant click-clack echoing off the players' studs on the concrete floor. From silence to clamour, from darkness out into bright floodlights.

Public announcer: Welcome to this Bnei Sakhnin home fixture. We've a big crowd here in Beit Shean tonight. Our opponents: the champions Maccabi Haifa. Until our Sons rise to the top, the club with the strongest Arab following. But don't expect a civil war . . .

True, many Arab fans are prepared to indulge themselves in a play of double allegiance – to Haifa and to Sakhnin. They seek to resolve the dilemma of split loyalties by convincing themselves that the Cinderellas in soccer boots will prove to be a passing episode. Such sceptics are in the minority. All around Arab communities all over Israel, The Sons have generated great excitement, great hope. They've become the 'national Arab team.' After all, Jewish fans support both Newcastle and England, so why can't an Arab fan in Israel support both Maccabi Haifa and Bnei Sakhnin? Now with Abbas and Abed Rabbah and Maccabi's Walid B'deir all in the Israeli national squad, questions of triple allegiance are arising (do English Jews have the same problem when England play Israel? Absolutely!).

Tonight, though, there are enough dilemmas with mere dual loyalties.

Many in the Haifa green resolve it by cheering loudly for both sets of players when they run on. Some have been cheering both teams so lustily that they can't cheer either any longer – they've lost their voices. So, too, the Beduin Boys Quartet, who've stationed themselves near The Gumble Trio as usual. They're voiceless too, from the hooting and chanting for The Sons all the way here. Their round trip from Rahat today is a full 360 miles. No matter if they can't sing, they're here to dance. Dance the full circle, here and back.

Before kick-off, the two teams assemble around the centre circle for a minute's silence. It's for Abbas's brother-in-law. He died suddenly the night before last, not long after the evening *Iftar* meal. His brother-in-law, also a cousin and a close friend, had a heart attack, aged 39. Abbas's sister is left with three small children, two of whom have mental handicaps. Abbas has been helping them out and now will be called upon to be even more of a support for the stricken family. He very nearly wasn't in tonight's line-up. A real dilemma – to play or not to play. Yesterday morning, a mourning tent had been set up in the cement courtyard surrounding the three blocs of flats of the Suan family. Among those who came to pay condolences is fitness coach Rosenberg. *Sotto voce* this time, he says he's not all that sure if Abbas is going to be able to leave the family-in-mourning to play the critical match. The club tells their captain, 'Do whatever you feel best – the ball's in your court'. When the line-up was announced a few minutes ago before the teams came out, you could hear the collective sigh of relief. The rumour that'd swept Sakhnin all afternoon that Abbas had decided to play proved true – he's here, in his customary No.8. This is an important game to win. Not only to assuage Abbas's personal grief. Securing three league points against the champions is *raison d'état*.

But Haifa are good, depressingly almost too good. At least we get to enjoy 15 minutes of grace. The boys are more than holding their own. A draw is usually unsatisfactory for any fan. Stay on level terms and tonight, dual loyalties won't be tested. The illusion is short-lived: the next half-hour shatters any hope of parity. By half-time, Sakhnin are three goals down. Abbas brings a moment of relief after the restart when he fires in a 20-yard drive. He falls to his knees, kisses the ground, in gratitude more than in triumph. No doubt there's also a little prayer. Only two more, murmurs Hilmi. Only two more, murmurs Abdullah. Only three more for those who want their dual loyalty issues solved once and for all. Again, the illusion is temporary, dual loyalty problems are easier dealt with than mesmerising Haifa forwards. They continue to overwhelm. Already, The Sons are missing Betar – it's becoming clear that if Betar didn't exist, Sakhnin would have to invent them. After the high emotion of Betar, it's been a rude crash landing. It's the same score as against Betar, only reversed. At the final whistle, believe it or not, Hilmi's pleased that it's only a 1-4 hammering: This season is no win-win mirage – to survive, we have to be realistic, to accumulate points, point by point. God willing next week.

A week later – Ramadan's into a third week – Sakhnin are back home in Beit Shean. Not only to recoup ground from the Haifa loss. But literally, if only temporarily, if only sporadically, to continue making the small tract of land – just 100-odd yards by 60 – theirs. The small Jewish town is not usually accustomed to being sensitive to Arab needs – to say the very least. A couple of years ago Sakhnin would have been greeted here with jeers and insults. Now they're most welcome.

An unlikely spirit of acceptance is growing between hosts and guests, between towns that used to reflect trenchant Israeli nationalism versus trenchant Arab nationalism. A decade or so ago, Beit Shean (population 15,000, compared to Sakhnin's 25,000) had a brief run at soccer glory themselves. Hapoel Beit Shean now languishes in the lower third of the fourth division. Out of the limelight, the host town console themselves by identifying with the new soccer underdogs, allies in discrimination, the shared feeling of those left far outside the winners' circle. But there's new hope. A brand new £12 million meat processing plant is opening with 200 new jobs in the offing. Understandably, no one in small town Beit Shean sneezes at that. Perhaps, it'll finally help close the gap between those who live on Israel's margins – literally geographically, and metaphorically. Sakhnin can only dream of a brand new factory with 200 new jobs.

There are still several days to the deadline for the £3.5 million *Sportoto* top prize on offer by the state-run football pools on the coming weekend's round of games. But at *Bis le-khol Kis* – 'A Bite for Every Pocket' – a shwarma joint that doubles as a *Sportoto* kiosk, young men and not-so-young are already filling out forms, clutching vain hopes of a sudden reversal in personal fortunes:

Hapoel Tel Aviv v Ashdod Sports Club – home away or draw, what d'yuh reckon?

Banker home win.
Screw Ashdod, they behaved so badly against Sakhnin.
Betar versus Bnei Yehuda?
Betar are struggling, give 'em only a draw.
Sakhnin-Maccabi Tel Aviv?
Let's go for our home team.
(Chuckles all round.)
Like us, they've got no real money.

'Dudu Surprise' is an out-of-work graduate in human engineering. He's playing for broke on his coupon: they are soccer from the bottom up − like us, they enjoy no *proteksia*. Israel's 'magical P word' − influence − is essential, not just to thrive, sometimes merely to survive. Dudu Surprise likes the fact that Sakhnin are also playing for broke: That Lachman, you've got to doff your hat, the way he makes the weak stand up against the strong. Once they were winning all their games. We liked that. Now, they've begun to lose too. You get the feeling that they're being battered, on and off the field, for who they are. Either way, they're good value for drama.

The undercurrent drama in little town Beit Shean is the switch of allegiance. No dual loyalties either: Beit Shean used to be Betar through and through. It's not so much that Betar are no longer all that successful − it's that they've been too successful for too long. Moved on and up in the world. The Jerusalem club is no longer seen as automatically representing people here, people who feel that the whole world is against them. In a curious kind of way, Sakhnin is gradually coming to fill that role − in Mundar's words, 'settling in peoples' hearts'. National identification and political differences are being relegated to a lower league of priorities, soccer the driving force soothing grievances of those left on the sidelines. Sakhnin's gaining acceptance on the fringes, becoming central to the periphery – even though they're Arabs: amazing isn't it?

Still more surprising is Beit Shean's surprise at its own change of heart. Hardened ex-Betar fans are suddenly joining in the condemnation of outbursts of racism against Sakhnin. Uri Suissa runs a sports goods store just a couple of doors away from *Bis lekhol Kis*: After what happened with Ashdod, I don't only want them to do well, I want any club which hammers them simply because they're Arabs to get hammered themselves. In football, there are no Jews, no Arabs – just football. That's what I say. Uri also has a personal bond. Sakhnin is now part of Beit Shean's extended family: I want Bnei Sakhnin to win because of 'Bibo' Avi Danan. Uri is the uncle of Linor, Bibo's wife: Bibo would never have developed in Beit Shean as he has in Sakhnin. Bibo local hero. From family affiliation to communal affiliation to soccer affiliation.

Tomer Eliyahu, his fellow centre back, remembers an hour with Bibo in Newcastle all too well. He had to work on him very hard to get him to play on the New Year holiday: Avi, come on, you can't just let us down – this is the game of our lives. Three seasons ago, after Beit Shean's fortunes slumped, Avi-Bibo, 29, made the move to Sakhnin 35 miles to the north-west – even before The Sons had earned their new national status. No, he doesn't see himself a pioneer. He simply grabbed the chance to make his mark in a team on the up. Upward social mobility through soccer, that's what it is. Without this club, I would never be where I am. He means to stay: I'm committed.

Bibo, dark-haired scion of a Moroccan immigrant family, sees no contradiction in playing another position – defender of the interests of both Beit Shean and Sakhnin. He's willing to serve as local advocate of both.

Suddenly, flying in to disturb the rosy picture, comes Charlton, boots and all. Charlton's the broadcasting company which has rights to all Israel's televised weekend matches. On this coming weekend they determined that Sakhnin should play their home fixture against Maccabi Tel Aviv on Friday afternoon, precisely at the time of the evening meal. The Sons plead for understanding: We don't mind playing during the fast, or after the fast. But fixing kick-off at precisely 4.30pm means that most of our fans simply won't make the 45-minute journey to Beit Shean. They'll have to break the fast at home and watch the game on TV. The fans will be let down, we'll be let down, and we'll lose a lot of gate money. Mazen seeks no special dispensation about not playing during daylight fasting hours. He isn't looking for any major sacrifice in Sakhnin's favour, he's merely looking for a bit of consideration. After all, wasn't Charlton compassionate enough only last week to shift a Betar Jerusalem kick-off time by an hour to allow the players and management the chance to attend the circumcision ceremony of the son of one of their club officials?

It's not affirmative action (or reverse discrimination) that Sakhnin wants – just equal treatment. Just a bit of respect. It comes back to the same old argument over Mazen's tactics of persuasion. Some believe their chairman should have been less conciliatory, more forceful, and insist that the IFA protect the interests and the sensitivities of one of its member clubs. You can't imagine that happening to another 'sector'. Once more, we have to face facts – we're not really *in*. Neither the chairman's popularity with the soccer authorities, nor his protests, nor even his gentle moral point about discrimination, get him anywhere. Kick-off time stays as declared.

Management fears are confirmed: There's almost no crowd for the 4.30pm ill-timed match. Instead of the usual Gumbul drums and cymbals, it's tomatoes, cucumbers, peppers and olives with which the 50-odd Sakhnin fans are armed, and with packets of pita bread on which to munch at half-time for their improvised *Iftar*. Some things never change, though: Hello, what's the problem? Mazen's neat diplomatic skills are again called into play. Along with their sandwiches, the faithful have brought bottles of water to quench their thirst at the end of the day of fasting. League regulations prohibit bottled drinks (even plastic bottles) into grounds for fear they'd be used as missiles should the crowd choose to vent its fury against errant refs. Mazen intercedes in the argument at the gates. The police are persuaded to allow a special Ramadan dispensation, once they hear Mazen's diplomatic compromise: all bottles will be opened before entry into the ground, the plastic tops confiscated, the missile head neutralised. Thanks *habibi*, thanks Shimon.

No fare in the stands, no fare on the pitch either. The game's almost as lean as the near-empty stands. It's great, this vacuous atmosphere – you can also hear the game.

Hear all the players calling out instructions to one another.

Hear Lachman thinking: Victory's the supreme value. You've got to pull several things together – character, endurance, commitment.

Hear Lachman smiting: 'Smite your enemy – before he smites you', indulging in a Talmudic exhortation popular among Jewish Israelis.

Hear Lachman barking:

Abbas get back into the middle.

Abbas don't get tempted by his moves!

Abbas!!!

Abbas, make sure everyone stays one-on-one all the time, don't lose them, I want close marking, dammit.

Abbas, what's happened to you today, your posture's all wrong! Fix it! You're so clumsy today.

Smarten up! Smarten up!

Hear Lachman talking to himself: That Abbas, I tell you, it's like talking to the wall. I don't know why I bother. Abbas!!

The game ends nil-nil. Sakhnin full back Ernest Etchi is sent off. More grist to the mill of the sports press and the TV sports shows for their now all-too-routine complaints about 'rough play'. Journalist Mahmoud Ghalia is more balanced, even if he is from Sakhnin: We about deserved to win – just about. But it's no good Sakhnin being marginally superior. We have to play at least 30 per cent better than the opposition to compensate for the stereotyped preconceptions which the refs now have of Lachman's tactics. There's a community feeling now among the refs. That's what accounts for their constantly harsh decisions against us. No way did Etchi deserve to be sent off.

Lachman isn't complaining: Never complain. Only the weak complain. Given the row over the kick-off time, I can live with a point. He looks at the result as one point gained, not two dropped. Anyway, the week after next there's an end-of-year break in the league – not because Ramadan is coming to an end.

Goals for Galilee

Christmas with the 'living stones'

Abuna (Father) Emile Ruhana pulls the sparkling green-and-gold garment over his customary black frock: last-minute preparations for the run-on to Christmas Morning Mass. The Christians of the Holy Land proudly project themselves as the 'Original Christians'. This morning's marking of Christmas in Abuna Emile's Greek Catholic church is in accordance with the Latin calendar. Their Greek Orthodox neighbours round the corner will only be celebrating their Christmas next week. Division rather than unity highlights the tiny Christian community here. 'Historic narrative is not what unites native Arab Christians,' writes Nazarene writer Atallah Mansour in his recently published *Narrow Gate Churches: The Christian Presence in the Holy Land under Muslim and Jewish rule*, 'Their story is not that of a closed, tightly knit or well-identified community; it is their future prospects and fears that bring them together as one tribe.'

Fears all right, but future prospects aren't so great. At least, not in terms of pure numbers. The Christian Arab population in the whole of Israel is barely 1.5 per cent, just over 100,000 altogether. A dwindling community facing permanent relegation, they're just 8 per cent of the Arab population. Here in Sakhnin, they're around 5 per cent. Atallah, a Maronite Catholic, berates his co-religionists from the West for 'abandoning the Holy Land's Christians', largely leaving them to their own devices and only caring about the holy sites – 'they should pay more attention to the plight of the "living stones".'

Here, at the top of Al Aqsa Martyrs' Street, virtually the entire Greek Catholic community of 800 souls – men, women, children and many babes in arms – has crowded into their new church, built with donations arranged by Abuna Emile from well-wishers in

Germany. Tribute to The Sons, the church is festooned in red-and-white garlands. The priest apart, and the fans apart, Eid Yamin, the club masseur, is the most notable representative of the ecumenical Sons here. This morning, his able hands are not banging disabled backs and thighs, but fondly cradling his little boy. He takes the boy's hand and teaches him how to cross himself – from right to left, the direction in which Arabic (and Hebrew) is written. There are plenty of other signs that the congregation is native: the Mass is strictly according to the rites of Rome, but it's all in Arabic. In contrast to Western churches, many men have their heads covered with a *keffiyeh* headdress while in prayer, hands are not held together and pointed vertically upward, but palms held upward, fingers curved into a bowl – similar to how hands are held in prayer within a mosque.

Across Martyrs' Street, down a narrow alley and around the corner, the mesmerising chants of the Greek Orthodox litany rise and fall. A regular Sunday service. Unlike the Greek Catholics who've largely been won over to the vernacular, the Greek Orthodox recite most of their prayers in the original Greek. In the little church, several icons bear the name of the Virgin Mary in Greek. It was back in 1715 that the 'Holy Land' Greek Catholics broke away from the Greek Orthodox, though they were forced to wait a century until getting official recognition for their Church from the temporal authorities of the Ottoman Empire. These days, it's level pegging in The Greeks (Catholics) versus The Greeks (Orthodox), both sides content with their 800–800 parity. Unlike in soccer, there are few transfers from one to the other.

Back in Christmas-time – in the other church around the corner – a parade of VIPs is fulfilling the time-honoured inter-communal tradition of honouring their minority.

Running on first – Sakhnin 'majority' leader, Abu Shadi. Mid-way through the Mass the mayor and a group of 'dignitaries' have trooped into a front row pew. Abuna Emile goes out of his way to respond to the gesture. He incorporates his warm welcome to the guests in his sermon. Later, in a festive reception in the church basement, everyone talks of positive interaction between 'our fraternal religions'. (For 'fraternal religions', read: Moslems and Catholics.)

Running on second – 'Super majority' representative, Superintendent Ilan Harush, recently installed as Misgav Regional Council police chief. The message of the new local top cop is similarly pacific: We're here to serve you. My door's always open. For me, Sakhnin is the most important place in our district. After all, you're our big town. Everyone understands he's going out of his way to show that gone is the hostility, the antagonism, which led up to October 2000. Today, a day when faith is unquestioned, when reconciliation is unquestioned, everybody takes him at face value.

It's not just the Christmas spirit. Sakhnin is no Nazareth – they're the real Nazarenes. There, over the Galilee hills in Nazareth, an unholy glow of Moslem-Christian tension is a constant. Not here, a town dedicated both to the profane (that is, to soccer) and to the holy (that is, to soccer). 'Tolerant but conservative.'

Israel has a Jewish majority, Sakhnin has a Moslem majority, the Greek Catholic and Orthodox are, in equal numbers, a minority within Sakhnin. But together as Christians, they're a minority within a minority, within Israel.

Chapter 8

Racism, Anthems and National Flags

Small-minded shrunken heads of political correctness

IT'S THE TALK OF THE TOWN – will Yevgeni Jok, who plays for Dinamo Minsk, be joining The Sons or not? The Sons are troubled. They're shaking up their playing staff. But the attempt to extricate themselves from a slippery slide into the dread red zone of relegation takes on a curious guise. A complex and sensitive manoeuvre is called for. The Jewish midfielder flew in last week. Bnei Sakhnin and Betar are competing to secure his services. But with the acquisition of a new Nigerian player, Audi Diok, The Sons already have their full complement of five foreign players. So the only way they can also sign the Minsk man is to apply The Law of Return. Now, The Law of Return is an Israeli fundamental, one of the first laws enacted by Israel soon after independence in 1948. The Law of Return guarantees the right of any Jew from anywhere in the world to immigrate to Israel and to obtain automatic citizenship. To qualify under The Law of Return, you're a 'Jew' if at least one of your grandparents is/was Jewish. Sakhnin is absorbing Jewish immigration, chuckle club officials at the neat way in which Mazen is trying to exploit what is for the Arab world, including Arab Israelis, one of the most contentious issues about the 'Jewish state'.

In short, if Yevgeni wants to play for the Arab club, the only way he can do so is if he's selected as a new Jewish immigrant under The Law of Return.

Sakhnin prides itself on shunting identity to the sidelines. But identity has been thrusting itself onto the Sakhnin pitch. Apart from one awkward goal in a friendly, Sakhnin striker Shlomo Edri hasn't scored once since the beginning of the season. Having failed yet again to score in defeat to Bnei Yehuda Tel Aviv, he trudges disconsolately off the field. There are more than the customary vigorous cries of frustration, 'Edri go home!' It's the undercurrent that's disturbing: one irate fan is heard muttering, only half to himself, our poor performances are again proof that the Jews don't really want us Arabs in the top league. The offensive catcalls bring immediate, and sharp, intervention from Abbas. A piercing stare from the captain, a wagged-finger warning to the hotheads to 'hold your tongues' and the wolves back off into their lair.

At the next training session, the wolves are out again. Edri is the butt of more abuse and derisive comment from fans who've come to watch how Lachman – only a couple of weeks ago 'our valiant tiger' – plans to extricate them from their misery. Of course, also to have a say about how they want it done. Fed-up-Edri retaliates in kind with insults of his own. It's the last straw. He pays the price. Maybe, on soccer merit, he deserves it. But the management insists on making a point: he's being let go, alright; he's being stripped of his Sakhnin identity, fine; but not because he's Jewish. Sakhnin's vaunted intercommunal harmony is tested to the full. But what the club is doing with its line-up has nothing to do with either national or communal identity – it's simply the soccer way. Now, 'The Brutal Law of Modern Soccer' dictates: success is all, failure demands decisive action. On this score, The Sons – whether adopting or abandoning – are definitely no exceptional soccer symbol.

On the other hand, whether they like it or not, Sakhnin is both symbol and reality. They are the touchstone of racism in Israeli soccer, and by extension, in Israeli society. For racism, read fierce assault on identity. At that same Bnei Yehuda match, whenever The Sons threatened to make a mark on the game, the chanting broke out: Only suicide bombers don't jump (Israeli fans indulge in the curious practice of not only standing and chanting for their team, but egging their heroes on by jumping up and down in unison on the edge of their seats). But there are also chants of: Death to Arabs. Before The Sons were born, Rifat 'Jimmy' Turk was the Arab icon of Israeli soccer. He was a star midfielder in the national team. Now, for both Arabs and Jews, he's the icon of anti-racism in Israeli soccer. The abusive chant has become so accepted that it's now acceptable as some sort of anthem Arab fans hear most in our soccer grounds.

But is 'Death to Arabs' more than downright racism? Does it have a semi-legitimate political component? After all, say some Jewish fans, Israel's at war, don't some Arabs want to wipe us out – you can't isolate the conflict from the stadiums. They have a point in arguing that you can't divorce soccer from society.

In Europe, 'Death to Arabs' would mean a ground closed, the

banning of the club – literally death to soccer. That's the last thing Sakhnin wants. Especially now that their new ground is at last being destroyed to make way for their home. A home where Sakhnin hope their sensitivities will be respected, a place where, in Abdullah's dream, even Betar fans will respond to hospitality in kind.

Africa out!

Wasn't it Woody Allen who said success is just disaster put on hold? To put looming disaster permanently on hold, you need excellence – is what the Jewish mother in an Allen film would say. Put into practice in Sakhnin, what you get is a Jewish mother in every Arab Son: Faith in excellence.

Oh what a beautiful morning! The larks, and even the crows, could be forgiven for breaking out in song on such a gorgeous winter day. How well it bodes for the all-important mid-table game against Hapoel Tel Aviv in Kiryat Eliezer. The Sons' management has decided to shift the game back to Haifa, both to break the Beit Shean jinx and, in the more mundane hope of replenishing the club's coffers, to attract a big turnout from their own supporters in Galilee and of visitors from Tel Aviv.

In his higgledy-piggledy living room, Mazen's hosting some of his Sons. There's a reason for the bash. It's meant to make the African players feel more at home. It's the idea of another key player, manager Lachman. Just this week, out of nowhere, No.1 Energy Murambadoro, the Zimbabwe national goalkeeper, informed Mazen that he won't be returning from 'a short trip' back to southern Africa where he'd gone for a World Cup qualifier. Left uncomfortably in the lurch, Mazen was at first inclined to brush off his ex-goalie's charge that he'd never been made to feel really at home. Still, Energy's desertion is a kind of own goal which threatens to stain the club's self-proclaimed identity as a miniature 'family of the world'. He was only a boy, you know, Lachman told Mazen, advising him to resort to his own well-tried tactic of *esprit de football*: I can only do as much as I can do – you've got to do your bit at bonding. Make them feel at home and they'll play like lions, run like giants, and we'll be king.

So here they are – Agoye Olomide, his wife and child all standing here in their colourful robes along with Ernest Etchi and Alain Massoudi, in the modest front room. The long yellow drapes in the Ghanaims's living room filter out the sunshine but they can't deflect the noise from the roundabout on 805 at the bottom edge of Martyrs' Street. Trophy after gleaming trophy of soccer triumphs are lined up, adorning the lounge.

Agoye: Which actually is the famous State Cup? I presume it's bigger than the Jules Rimet Trophy. Isn't it amazing that they made the original World Cup so small?

Mazen: I hope we can come down to Africa in 2010 to watch Israel versus Nigeria in the final.

Agoye: Is this it?

Mazen: Let me show you this one: I particularly treasure this one – we won it for fair play. We'd like to keep it permanently.

Lachman: Fair play, okay, but tough fair play.

Fair play – tough or soft – it's soon gonna blow up in their face.

Oh, what a beautiful evening! Red-and-white larks indeed burst into song: Hapoel *ole, ole!* drenches both sides of the pitch. This game is an all-important mid-table clash but, after all, aren't we all friendly enemies in tune with the same song – Hapoel United unite!

Oh my God – did we bring the match ball? Jamal! Where's the ball? Mazen's never been seen in a tizzy before. Don't worry boss, it's already with the ref in his dressing-room, I made sure he doesn't have anything to complain about, that fancy pants – Lachman reckons that beneath that dandyish demeanour of his, that referee Asaf Keinan's a real bastard.

It was all going very well, actually. Just after the half hour, Hapoel's goalkeeper, Ahmad Kassoum, heads home right through Sakhnin's hands. The Sons are ahead, *Oleh, oleh!* But then, just before half-time, the songs turn into jeers: the referee sends Etchi for an early shower after the big centre-back picks up a second yellow for an innocuous foul. The Sons hold on to their one goal advantage; the visitors are silent.

The Sons are in full flow again when Keinan blows for the re-start. But within a minute, they fall silent. Meir Cohen, the No. 2 keeper, is in goal for Sakhnin. Cohen's only able to parry a fierce long-distance shot and the Tel Aviv striker Ibezito Ogbonna pounces to slide home from close range. It's all jitters in the home stands now; and, it gets even worse. Five minutes later, a perfectly weighted cross from the right sees another African Hapoel player, John Pantsil, storming in from the defence to hammer the ball past the hapless Cohen.

1-2 behind.

What a miserable debut the substitute keeper's having! He should've been invited this morning too! And what's with our Africa today? Energy's missing, Etchi's sent off, Agoye's lost while Ogbonna and Pantsil are turning this sunny day into a freezing winter hell!

Tel Aviv, singing; Sakhnin, still.

But on the pitch, things are anything but still. Because of Keinan's bias, The Sons so lost it that they began kicking just about anything that moved – except the ball. It gets worse when, two minutes before the end, Massoudi scythes down Abutbul and the referee leaves Sakhnin to play injury time with no African players (except Agoye) and only nine men. Actually, there's no injury time this time – everybody's already bruised, or sent off. Nine against eleven, 1-2. Oh what a lousy evening!

Some of the Sakhnin supporters respond by throwing (uncapped) plastic bottles and generally go on a bit of a rampage. Lachman and the rest of the Sakhnin bench, even Mazen huddling on the touchline, are all seething at Keinan, red-and-white in their anger. The ref goes off, escorted by his two linesmen and a veritable phalanx of policemen. Suddenly, a big lout with a bushy moustache comes storming up and starts remonstrating angrily with Keinan. Moustache wags his index finger right in his face. The ref reels back. Was he hit? From now on for the next three days, that's the only question that echoes through the national headlines – DID SAKHNIN HIT THE REF? (Moustache is later identified as a part-time Sons' man.) It's claimed that the ref needed to go to hospital to treat his injuries.

Next morning, Mazen has to drive back to Haifa to give evidence to the police. He's told by Superintendent Shimon that there's no proof of Keinan's allegation. Either nobody saw or nobody's willing to corroborate that an assault took place. In addition, there are no physical signs on the referee's face that would indicate he was punched.

The FA disciplinary committee rules that the bully's banned from all soccer grounds for the coming two seasons and Sakhnin are compelled to play two games without a crowd and fined 30,000 Shekels. You got off lightly – we're applying affirmative action, the court tells Mazen. His public posture is that this is a heavy burden on a small club.

But privately, in the confines of the higgledy-piggledy living room, Mazen's relieved.

The fervent fan sees all . . . with a little help from his friends (and a radio)

Sakhnin is self-reliance. Taysir Hasqiyah is self-reliance incarnate. He's even learnt not to rely on Sakhnin. They're losing too often, may their father's chest bones stew! Still, he can't stop loving them.

Today, we're away in Petah Tikva. It's important not to fall into a depression just because we got a nasty hammering and the FA disciplinary committee came down on us with a heavy hand just because of a slight tap on the ref's shoulder – but we don't want to talk about that anymore do we? Long live away games! Sakhnin, *Oleh, oleh!*

Sakhnin! Sakhnin! Sakhnin! God willing, victory – only victory. We're not leaving without victory! We're not moving unless we win! That's not just a hope. Victory for certain.

Sakhnin have been given the sunny side. The sun dips low in the winter glow, accentuating the crimson of Taysir's T-shirt and of his crimson (from constant shouting) face. His booming voice carries all the way across the pitch. He's not quite synchronised, though, with the 'Red's rising, Red's rising' chant that unites the rest of the crowd. Taysir's big and burly behind his big black sunglasses. As usual, a multi-task force all on his own. He manages, all at once, to chain smoke; yell down to his men (alternatively, instructions and support) – 'C'mon Tomer!'; curse the opposition – 'Salim Toameh, you dog!'; listen to the commentary through the small transistor radio, which nestles between shoulder and ear; chew sunflower seeds; spit out their skins; smoke another half-pack of Marlboros.

It's tough to coordinate a whole team of derelict players even if you're blessed with a broad frame. When his shirt comes off in the warm winter sun, Taysir doesn't try to hide his beer-belly gut below the chequered-red Sons' scarf that he keeps loyally in place through all the heat of the game. The belly comes from another source – drinking is one field in which Taysir plays strictly by the rules – a hard coke is as much as he and his brethren will indulge: I'm here to be part of our victory. Being close with our team makes me happy. I'm among my people, my family. We're all one family, one home.

Every now and again, he adds another element to his repertoire, reaching over to grab a giant red flag from the young man besides him. His young colleague hands it over without taking his eyes off the action. Sullenly, Taysir returns it when the butt of his curses, Salim Toameh, justifies all the attention that Taysir has been paying him: Salim Toameh, you son-of-a-bitch! Petah Tikva's quicksilver striker has just put the hosts ahead. Salim's an Arab brother. Mazen couldn't have him as a Son. Not for want of trying – I wish we'd had the means.

All the while, the radio-in-ear remains embedded between shoulder and ear. Taysir comments on the radio commentary. He needs to reassure himself that's he got his analysis right, or is it simply the deafening commentary that's blotting out his own thoughts? Either way, Hell, at last we're attacking, c'mon! Let your father be cursed! Hell, he missed. Like a TV replay, Taysir repeats what all the other brothers have just seen.

Taysir, what's the Beersheba score? (They too have a critical game and could be fellow relegation stragglers.)

Still nil-nil. They're still not losing. It's nil-nil, I'm afraid.

There's a more prosaic reason than being blind for Taysir's radio implant: Sure, the radio helps us to keep up with the other games, who else is winning, who's losing. Take the flag, will you. Dammit, Hapoel Haifa are now ahead, and we are . . . well, you know what's happening with us – Taysir understatement for still trailing and, frankly, looking very much like going further behind, and it's not yet half-time and you know what will happen to us in the second half, unless . . .

But it's hard to faze Taysir: In five minutes, we'll score, you'll see. We'll equalise. I feel it in my bones. Salim Toameh, curse your father's chest bones!

Two-nil. Dammit! Disaster. Petah Tikva have scored again. And, who else but that renegade ass Salim Toameh – so what if, this time, it's only an assist.

Poor Taysir gets the kick in his teeth twice: He hears the clamour of the Petah Tikva fans drowning out the desolate silence on his side of the ground and then seconds later the delayed goal-flash on the radio. Taysir tries to bury his anguish. Still, he stays loyally in the game. Until he can finally take no more. He pockets the radio, and challenges: When will this damn story be over?

Three-nil.

No longer silence. Even with the radio switched off, the desolation's all too audible. The Sons are hit by a rain of angry chants, a downpour of accusative finger-pointing, a monsoon of insulting finger-raising: Rub-bish! Rub-bish! Rub-bish!

Even Gumbul's drums have fallen silent. But Gumbul isn't silenced. He unleashes a torrent of enraged staccato abuse: Dissolute sons-of-bitches! Call yourselves players – sons-of-bitches the lot of you, every single one of you! Leave me alone, for God's sake! He shrugs off a would-be friendly arm of consolation of a bruised brother-in-arms. He runs up the perimeter fence, shaking it furiously to vent his anger on his erstwhile giants from as close as he can get. It's a good thing the IFA regulations about bringing down perimeter fences haven't reached Petah Tikva yet. The anger grows. It becomes more unrestrained. There's spitting through the fence. A troupe of policemen positions itself – just in case. But the anger is mostly self-inflicted.

A sprinkling of groupies of the Beduin Boys Quartet from Rahat try to rally spirits by unfurling the blue-and-white Star of David. One of them waves the flag and then wraps it around his neck like a super scarf. Someone comes over to remonstrate quietly. There's a short discussion. The flag is folded, packed away and sat on: They don't want us to show the flag. Some don't want us to fly the flag at all. We want to – why not? It's our country. We wanna fly it, so what? What's the problem? I don't see the problem. We play in the Israeli League, don't we? If they don't want to show the flag, why play in the country at all?

Five minutes before the final whistle, hand on his flag-holder's shoulder, Taysir is trudging disconsolately away. Their enormous red flag trails dismally in the dust behind them.

Flags are actually unusual here. Unlike fans in many countries, for all their passion, the Bnei Sakhnin supporters almost never fly flags – neither the Israeli colours nor the Palestinian colours, nor even Sakhnin flags most of the time. It's as if soccer success allows them to be Israelis without having to raise the Israeli flag, just as it allows them to be Palestinians without sporting the Palestinian flag. When The Sons win they raise the flag (with or without permission), but only when they beat 'the national enemy' – Betar Jerusalem.

The battle of the Chosen Peoples

A bitingly bitter Jerusalem winter evening. An unwelcoming night at Teddy Stadium, Betar's home ground. Betar are desperate to avenge that 4–1 drubbing in Haifa. Sakhnin are anxious to preserve the validity of their new altarpiece, a spectacular banner heralded by the Hebrew word 'humiliation' and adorned by their red-and-white Arab stallion perched on a football trampling underfoot Betar's black-and-yellow menorah. The Sakhnin stands relish the symbol. Ninety minutes from now, they hope to relish the result. The Betar hardcore are at it again, cursing the Arabs, cursing the Prophet. Not that some of The Sons' boys don't give every much as good as they get. Their jibes are also pretty provocative, sometimes downright nasty, but less offensive. Mostly, tongue-in-cheek, pre-emptive: 'Terrorists! Terrorists!' is the taunt intercepting the 'Suicide Bombers! Suicide Bombers!' which Betar have volleyed at them.

'Bnei Sakhnin at war!'

All of a sudden – a moment of grace. So it seems. A moment of friendliness. A moment of togetherness. Sakhnin-Betar brothers-in-arms:

Jews and Arabs! Arabs and Jews!
Jews and Arabs! Arabs and Jews!

Brothers-in-arms? Hard to believe.On closer inspection, it's actually brothers-at-each-other's-throats. Again. As always. What they're actually singing is not 'Jews and Arabs and Arabs and Jews' but 'Jews *of* Arabs! Arabs *of* Jews!' It's the Betar chant. If nasty, quite sophisticated. They're targeting Jewish players playing for Arab Sakhnin and also intimating that, in fact, Sakhnin Arabs are nothing more than lackeys serving their Jewish masters. They don't want an Arab club in their league, they'll never have an Arab player in their club, many of them wouldn't want Arabs in the country at all.

One-nil to Sakhnin.

There's no mistaking the theological purpose of what's becoming a real soccer chart-topper: *Allahu akbar*! God is greatest! What lifts the Beduin Boys Quartet cheerleaders is that they not only rap '*Allahu akbar*!', they wrap it in the blue-and-white Star of David. This time, no debate, no argument about the flag. The flag's *halal*. This time, the Israeli colours are proudly on display, proudly and to stay. Perhaps to neutralise accusations of dirty play from the Betar camp – the charge that Sakhnin's a 'Fifth Column'.

The Beduin Boys Quartet are in no way disconcerted:

We raise the flag, we also say: *Allahu akbar*. With God's help, we've come to win. And, with God's help, we *will* win!

Two-nil.

[*Groupies' Chorus*]

God the greatest!

God the greatest!

God the greatest!

The chant tumbles into a dance of joy. A victory dance.

> Two more, God willing!
> [*Groupies' Chorus*]
> Five, with God's help! *Hamsa*!
> Four-nil! Four, we don't need more.
> Yeah, let's be optimistic, four's enough.

They sweep into a traditional Beduin song:

> Welcome the guests all,
> With sword and saber held high!

'Teddy' is swept away. Two young men break deliriously into a Sabbath song favoured by Yemenite Jews:

> Tonight, tonight,
> Great rejoicing tonight.

'Teddy' is dancing. Bare-chested Gumbul is oblivious to the cold, oblivious to his own heat. Surreally, the smoke of his sweat and the vapour from the heavy-breathing man upon whose shoulders he's precariously perched stand out against the moonless night.

Betar *Salama* – Goodbye Betar, goodbye! And not *au revoir*. O Betar, you whore! A young woman, clad in yellow-and-black is led away by the cops. She gesticulates wildly. Sakhnin roars approval. Up, up, up go a phalanx of unholy middle fingers. Whore! Whore! Whore! No pity for the Betar diehards who choose to endure the final agony. They endure more taunts:

Go home already! Enough of you!
Down to the Third Division you go!

It's tonight's only false call. It's surely not in their interests to have Betar relegated. In the two encounters this season against the Jerusalem team, The Sons have played out of their skins. Tonight's win at 'Teddy' has made it two victories, two draws, one defeat since last season when The Sons won the right to battle Betar in the top league. If only the season was made up solely of series of Sakhnin v Betar matches, The Sons would surely be runaway league leaders.

Final whistle, all together now:

God exists!
Arabs exist!

Tonight, they've silenced the traditional Betar chant, 'God exists, Arabs don't exist.' Tonight, they feel *they* are the Chosen People.

Chapter 9

Abbas, Hero of Israel

Our boy keeps Israel's World Cup dream alive

JEWISH ISRAELIS LOVE to believe that they're self-reliant. Not in the sense of the myth of the individualistic spirit of the pioneer from which Americans love to believe they're forged; more in terms of a collective aspiration not to be dependent on others for national existence.

Translated to the Suans, self-reliance usually involves commitment to Sakhnin's soccer fortunes. But, because of their identification with their son – first among equals of The Sons – and his recent inclusion in the national team, commitment now means absolute loyalty to Israel's soccer destiny: Israel can rely on 'our Abbas'. Just give us a chance. Give us a chance to give you a chance.

It's hard playing at home. In the living room, final preparations before kick-off. Abbas's wife Safa's just tucked-in four year-old Mabsam. Little Muhammad, dressed for the national party in Sakhnin red-and-white pyjamas, insists on spending the match in his mother's arms. He's balanced precariously under one arm as she returns from the kitchen with several bottles of water. They're snapped up quickly. Brothers, cousins, nephews and nieces take their assigned places in the small parlour. They'll need a lot of sustenance to see them through the coming 90 minutes. The Suans' stands are few straight hard-backed chairs. Cushions and mattresses set in a semicircle on the floor are the VIP boxes. In the standing section at the back, a couple of teenage girls giggle to themselves alongside Safa and Little Muhammad.

Voice of Meir Einstein (Israel TV commentator): Welcome to the national stadium in Ramat Gan. A crunch match tonight against the Republic of Ireland. World Cup qualifier, European Group 4. A tough group, Shlomo?

Voice of Shlomo Sharf (Israel TV soccer analyst, former national team manager): A tough group, indeed, Meir. But, so far, the national team have more than held their own.

Einstein: Who would have imagined that after four rounds we'd still be level with the favourites – France and Ireland?

Sharf: Avram Grant has his critics – I can even admit I'm one of them – but you've got to say Grant has done well: France, Ireland, Israel – eight points apiece. Whatever happens tonight, Grant's men have already done well. But tonight, the French are in the Stade de France hosting Switzerland. We can expect them to take all three points there.

Einstein: That puts even a bigger burden on Avram's boys tonight. Israel simply has to win or, at least, not to lose. There's an awful lot hinged on this game . . . a fateful evening, we can safely say that.

Issam (Abbas's older brother No.3): Come on, if it's so fateful, why don't they give Abbas a chance?

Abbas, Hero of Israel

Sa'id Hamad Suan (Abbas's dad): I prayed he'd start tonight. At least he's on the bench.

Mohammed (Abbas's older brother No.6): Patience, dad, patience. He looked good in the warm-up though, didn't he? Maybe Grant will still come to his senses.

No snacks, no coffee even. Spartan conditions. No trivial distractions permitted. Only water, and only in plastic bottles. Caps are allowed. The match is the thing.

[. . .]

Einstein: Keane . . . Keane to Kilbane . . . He moves down the left. This is dangerous stuff. Over here on this side, Israel's looking exposed. Watch out! The cross comes in. Morrison. Oh my goodness, it's there – Ireland one, Israel nil.

Sharf: The way our defence is shaping up, that was expected. A real blow just two minutes before half time.

Silence in the little living room. Shock. Issam clicks his fingers, motioning for another bottle of water. He unscrews the little blue plastic cap. He takes a big gulp. Hard work this – living the game.

Ahmad, Abbas's eldest brother No.1, lounges back into the cushions, he looks half-asleep. But his left hand suspended motionless in the air is a giveaway: He can't move from the game.

[. . .]

Einstein: This is better from Israel now. Yossi Benayoun. Cuts through, passes one defender, and another. This could be useful.

[*Whistle*]

Issam: Red! Red! That deserved a red card. Come on ref, really.

Omar (Abbas's older brother No.4): Have some water.

Ahmad: (Left hand suspended motionless in the air.)

Sharf: That *was* cynical. A tackle from behind. Keane could easily have picked up a red. He certainly deserved that yellow.

At half-time, Safa slips out to put Little Muhammad to bed. She's still calm. In adversity, she still believes . . .

Einstein: You know Shlomo, we may still be trailing, but overall, that wasn't half a bad half. There's plenty of promise, it seems to me, and there's still a full 45 to go.

Sharf: Promise, well yes, to some extent. And, it's true that Grant's got some useful assets on the bench. Let's see what he does with them. What I miss is a bit of inspiration . . .

Issam: So what's he waiting for? Bring Abbas on.

Alia (Abbas's sister no.1, praying feverishly non-stop from the opening whistle): *Ya Rab! Ya Rab!* O God! O God!

Einstein: . . .Or a spot of divine intervention.

[. . .]

Abdallah (Abbas's older brother no.5): GOAL! GOAL! We're level.

Sa'id Hamad: B'deir, B'deir, Walid's scored!

Issam and Mohammed (*in unison*): BA-DEIR! BA-DEIR! BA-DEIR!

Safa: (Squeaks of joy.)

Einstein: Wait a minute, Ivanov's disallowing it. Can't be! Can it? I didn't see what was the infringement – was there any?

Sharf: I'm not sure either. But this Russian ref has long been a thorn in our side. Let's see that replay . . .

Omar: Hey, that ball was over the line – one hund-dred per cent. Look, see . . . maybe.

All: We need some more water over here.

Ahmad: (Left hand suspended motionless in the air.)

[. . .]

Issam: This is it. At last, Abbas is coming on. *Yalla* Abbas! Let's show 'em.

Einstein: Let's go down to Shlomi on the touchline near the national bench. I see Grant's preparing a change. Who's coming on as substitute?

Shlomi: Yes Meir, it's Omer Golan who's coming off and . . . Suan who's on. No.19, Abbas Suan.

Sharf: I must say I'm really not sure about this change. Why pull out a striker for a midfielder?

Einstein: A defensive midfielder at that.

Mohammed: *Ya Rab*, give him a chance. There's only quarter-of-an-hour left. What's Grant got to lose?

Alia: *Ya Rab, ya Rab!*

Safa: (A quiet smile.)

[. . .]

Hands clasped.

Feet in full flight.

Sharf: He deserved a yellow card for that tackle. You can say one thing about Suan — he doesn't mince his words, nor his tackles.

Einstein: That's two cards the Sakhnin man has picked up in successive games. That means he's out against France next week. Also, it doesn't help tonight's cause. The injured Irishman's clearly happy to eat up every precious second, getting attention on the ground after that tough tackle.

Sharf: It wasn't smart of Suan. Perhaps his only excuse is he's trying too hard. To prove a point. He's clearly still smarting from the way he was taunted in Jerusalem during the friendly there against Slovenia a couple of weeks ago.

Einstein: That was a disgrace the way some Betar Jerusalem

fans booed and jeered. You just can't say 'an Arab has no place in the national team'.

Sharf: You're right, Meir. Still, it doesn't excuse Suan playing dirty. Recklessness is not what Israel needs right now.

Issam: What do they want of us? Hundred per cent effort isn't enough?

Omar: Pass the water.

[. . .]

Psalm 151

Einstein: We're into injury time now. Still one-nil down. There's the board, Ivanov has signalled three additional minutes. Is there time for a last minute reprieve? Who's going to provide salvation?

Sharf: The way things are going, I just can't see it.

Einstein: A minute over the 90, less than two to go. Wait a sec. Yossi Benayoun . . . Benayoun down the left, could this be promising? Benayoun to Yaniv Katan, Katan. Katan leaves it, what on earth's he doing? Katan lets it go, to Suan. Suan . . . he strikes it . . . hard. GOD, IT'S THERE. SUAN . . . SUAAAAN, Abbas Suan has done it! He's done it!

Ireland one, Israel one. This is amazing . . . absolutely amazing!

Ahmad: (Left hand suspended motionless in the air.)

Safa: (A little quiver of joy. Soprano squeak. Big broad smile.) He's done it. She knew he would. I always knew he would.

Sharf: Amazing, simply amazing. A goal from 20 metres, a goal from nowhere. Shay Given had no chance. What a goal!

Einstein: A God-given goal. Abbas is on his knees. He kisses the turf, a prayer. Everybody kisses him. My, how he deserves it.

Mohammed: *Ya Rab*, shut up, already, here's the replay: What a shot, what a shot, what a screamer. Our little brother . . . our little brother for the national team.

Sa'id Hamad: The V sign. We did it. An Arab did it. We've saved Israel.

Alia: *Ya Rab*! Abbas has brought God onto Israel's side. Thanks be to God.

Einstein: I confess I can't remember when I was so excited. A mythical goal.

Sharf: Meir, we're just hearing that in Paris, France have been held goalless by the Swiss! Abbas's point means we're still very much in the race. If I'm not mistaken the draw here means that, on goal difference, we're actually in second spot – beg your pardon, I'm so excited I'm getting ahead of myself – we're still behind the French but equal on points . . .

Einstein: Hang on Shlomo, we've got Shlomi down on the touchline with Abbas. Shlomi?

Shlomi (*Breathless*): Abbas, your reaction, bless you.

Abbas: Before you start blessing me, I want to bless the whole of Israel and to wish everyone a happy holiday. I dedicate my goal to this being a very happy Purim. It's a very important holiday for the Jewish people and for the State of Israel (*choking back tears*). I was very hurt by what happened in Jerusalem with the Betar fans. I've had a very difficult couple of weeks. I was confident, I knew I could do it, but I confess, I didn't believe that I'd score such a vital goal for Israel.

Shlomi: What did you say in your prayer?

Abbas: Straightaway I kissed the ground. I wanted to thank God for granting me this great privilege – to score my first goal for the national team in such an important game. My biggest dream is to get to the World Cup Finals. After that, I don't know if there'd be anything left to dream about. I give thanks to God that he's given me the chance to prove once more that in the State of Israel we're all one people, united as one single person. Enough already, this talk of Jews, and of Arabs. We're one country, and we're all in it together.

No Arabs, no World Cup, and this is the guy Lachman criticised for poor posture?

Avram Grant prefers a more prosaic explanation: Ireland took off a striker. I looked for a sub capable of shooting from a distance who, at the same time, can latch on to loose balls out of their defence, or pushed up from ours. Suan's the only defensive midfielder in the country who marshals a match and shoots effectively from far. He convinced me that he deserved the chance. He's done everything I asked of him. I don't ask for more.

In six weeks time, Israel will be marking Independence Day. The goal has brought the national celebration fast forward. Abbas's declaration sounds like one of the patriotic pledges made by the 12 honoured citizens chosen to kindle 12 beacons (for the XII Biblical Tribes of ancient Israel) in the ceremony that ushers in Independence Day celebrations. Has Abbas ushered in a new era – are the Arabs about to be accepted as the Thirteenth Tribe of Israel?

The mayor's assistant Ghazal calls it a 'goal of acceptance'. Mundar translates the last-gasp equaliser literally, 'a goal for equality'. For Sa'id Hamad Suan, it's much more than equality. It's the sign of victory: victory for Israel, victory for the Jews of

Israel, victory for the Arabs of Israel. Above all, victory of the Arabs of Israel over the Jews of Israel, over the way Israel relates to the Arabs of Israel. Sakhnin is heaven. The Suans' is the gateway. A pilgrimage place. Congratulations fly in all directions: 'A shot against racism', 'A volley into the Jewish Israeli camp', 'A magical shot' garland the stream of well-wishers. Mohammed, Abbas's older brother No.2, greets them: Everything's different now. Abbas Senior greets them: Well, maybe different, but only if *they* change. We've done our bit for acceptance. Now it depends on them, on what they do, on how they take things from here.

But it's not the pessimists, nor even the pepsimists, but the optimists who are top dogs tonight – the believers that the goal will inspire a sea change. The relationship may, or may not, change as a result of the goal. But already, you get a sense that Abbas's position in the team has definitely changed. It's not just that his goal has already become a symbol. Abbas himself is being transformed into a national icon. Will he change?

The goal's still reverberating. Sakhnin's gathering again, not around the pitch or the TV set, but on the streets. It's Land Day – the second painful memorial day on Sakhnin's political calendar. Not a spring festival in celebration of land, when land comes alive, but an anniversary marking the loss of land, when memory of the dead comes alive. For the second time this season, the same crowd has assembled at the same memorial in the old cemetery on Main Street where the dead of both Land Day and the 'October Events' are buried. There's little evidence of The Sons and their fans. Most here believe more in politics than in soccer. Like Trees Kosterman, a Dutch woman married to Ali

Zubeidat, the Sakhnin distributor of English textbooks, very much a political activist. The Abbas moment isn't lost on her; of course she watched the match: I don't really care about soccer. I was out and came back just before the end of the game. My daughter said 'Mum, come quickly. Abbas, he's just come on!' I'm glad I didn't miss it. That goal – it's so, so significant. Maybe, we can just build on it. How much is Israel's World Cup dream saved by Abbas worth?

Land, ground and holy shrines

Inside City Hall, Ibrahim Haleileh, one of Mayor Abu Shadi's deputies whose special brief it is to follow land matters, is just completing his midday prayer. Mecca is to the south-east of Galilee's soccer mecca. On the south-east wall of his small office, a true-to-life picture of the Kaaba in Mecca; on the western wall, a truer-than-life virtual poster of Sakhnin's 'shrine' – the way the new stadium will look when it's real; and, on the north-west wall, a map of the hills and valleys that surround Sakhnin, facing Mecca. Ibrahim tilts up from his prayers to lay out grievances on the map. He sweeps a broad swathe of purple – the large tracts of confiscated lands: Over several decades, we've been handed several red cards. They're all about land expropriation. In 1964, we lost land in the Bet Netofa valley south of Sakhnin for the National Water Carrier project. Then, in the '70s, the area known as 'Zone 9' went for an army training area. In the early '80s, it was the large Raphael arms development base on the hill.

In 1991, the Torodyon Hill became the Misgav Industrial Park. Finally, in May 1999, they opened the army base that sits right on top of our heads. All were built on land that was once Sakhnin's. That last 'red card' has been the most galling. Not only is the base 'right on top of our heads', we were never told the purpose for which that large tract of land was taken away. Naively, we thought they were going to put up a big park. Unfortunately, on this field of land, red cards tend to be permanent. Our dream is that the country at last seriously addresses our land needs. Why do you think we keep on and on with Land Day? Do you think people would be in the streets today? Why do they demonstrate? Is it any fun? It's no fun!

The blunting of the land dream partly explains why Sakhnin is so wrapped up in the practical dream of building their new stadium. Seven million shekels (around £1 million) has been earmarked by various government sources – half that sum by the Prime Minister's Office. It's the fulfilment of the promise Ariel Sharon gave on that May night when they lifted the Cup.

Abu Shadi suddenly pops in, summons us to his office, bubbling from a meeting he's just had in Jerusalem, wants to report encouraging news immediately – about one very specific patch of ground, *the* Ground. 'Encouraging?' all very fine, argues his ever-pessimistic deputy. But the mayor's already moved on to spread the good news. He's out of earshot, his 'good news' echoing through the corridors of City Hall drowns out Ibrahim's reservations: Completing the ground renovation in no way tackles our acute land shortage.

Two flags are tacked to the sloping roof over the mayor's head – the municipal flag and the national flag. On the wall behind, amid a galaxy of the customary soccer trophies and coexistence mementoes (is the Cup one of them?), two photographs – one of the President and one of the Prime Minister. At the other end of the room, photographs of the two Sakhnin men killed in October 2000, their pictures partially covered by the victorious Daughters of Sakhnin, the under-18s who were national girls' champs in the same year. An equaliser between the Daughters and The Sons.

There's a trail of townsfolk at the mayor's door. At the end of her long painted nails, Abu Shadi's trusted secretary, Wafiqa Ghanaim, has her hands full keeping the grievances at bay – a house threatened with demolition, a prolonged electricity stoppage in a small factory, a roof leaking in an overcrowded kindergarten. But Abu Shadi won't allow his jolly mood to be spoiled. Finally, he's released himself, temporarily, from the vicissitudes of the job to focus on what really would change his town – locking up the necessary funds for the stadium. He thought of saving the good news from Jerusalem as future political capital but he can't help trumpeting his delight. After the three-hour drive back to his home turf, confined with his news, he's breathless: With the State Budget now safely through, senior officials in the Prime Minister's Office are promising us an additional half-a-million pounds over and above the million which they've already transferred to help complete the first phase of the revamping of the Stadium. Now, it's almost a given that we'll be ready for the dedication at the start of next season. I hope we can get the Prime Minister to come in person to kick it off.

In the Tora Bora hide-out

The French and Israeli players are just beginning to line up at Ramat Gan for the anthems. Eyes are not yet on the big screen near the bar. The click–click of the balls on the tables goes on uninterrupted. The Tora Bora billiard hang-out is jocularly named after the hide-outs deep in the Afghan mountains. Appropriately, Tora Bora's a cavernous joint, rather stylish in the dim lights that blaze directly above the four green baize tables. The opening whistle of the first World Cup qualifier after the last World Cup qualifier – the ground-zero Abbas game – draws near. More and more of the billiard boys set their cues aside and line up around the set. No one joins in the national anthem. But through the haze of *nargileh* smoke, there's distinct new hope. Omar Hayadry opened Tora Bora just two months ago as one of the very few places where Sakhnin's young men can go: Tonight, everyone's rooting for Israel. Now, that's remarkable. Take me, for instance – for the first time in my life, I definitely want Israel to win. I've always backed France before because of Zinedine Zidane. I've always identified wholeheartedly with French fortunes. But our Abbas has changed it all. For the first time, we're feeling part of Israel.

Unlike Omar, Jewish Israelis have a very troubled attitude towards the French. They love to hate them because of the way they see the French 'cosying up to the Arabs'. Precisely why Omar liked 'Les Bleus'. So tonight, on top of the national agenda, it's no longer the customary suspicions towards Arab Israelis and why they don't sing *Hatikvah*, but whether Jewish Israelis will behave themselves during *La Marseillaise*. A turn-up for the book: Not that the Arab players sing, but that the Jewish fans boo. They shouldn't do that, they really shouldn't do that. Omar feels comforted, for once, to be more respectful to matters of anthems. He boos when a section of the blue-and-white crowd at the National Stadium in Ramat Gan jeer the French anthem.

Back at the Suans'

The second half gets underway at the National Stadium. Still nil-nil, although the French are making mincemeat of Israel. They could well have been three or four goals to the good. Our brother isn't playing because of that damn second yellow card he picked up in the Irish game. But their faith hasn't failed. The Suans believe in soccer miracles. Maybe, there'll be a replay of the magical moment. Maybe, another of the Arab players will be tonight's national saviour.

Just three minutes into the half, despair threatens, thickens. Israeli goalie, Dudu Awat, commits a howler. Israel go behind. A low moan from Issam: What a terrible mistake!

All's not yet lost, hold thumbs at home, answers the national soccer exhorter, Meir Einstein.

We're holding all right, holding hard, responds uncle Dibb.

G-O-A-L.

Off guard, the family leap to their feet as one. Walid B'deir has headed home another unlikely equaliser, the second inside a week. It's one apiece. An Arab player has again managed to keep Israel's World Cup dream warm. Safa La Passionaria leads the electrified home crowd: five minutes still to go. Avram bring on our Abed Rabbah! You know you can count on Sakhnin. He'll do what Abbas did.

Avram Grant ignores the plea. It stays 1-1.

Before being called to national duty again, the Suans will be on Sakhnin duty. Abbas and Abed Rabbah will again be playing. It's Betar time once more.

Abbas, Hero of Israel

Mahmoud's dream nightmare

Journalist, Mahmoud Ghalia is a soccer nationalist. Soccer's his supreme commitment. As an Arab nationalist, he hopes soccer will score where politics has missed. On the other hand, Mahmoud hates soccer – for 'killing our politics'. He hates soccer because it gives an illusion of equality – there's equality only for the 90 minutes. On the other hand, Mahmoud hates politics because it doesn't change anything. On the other hand, because of his politics, one thing's for sure – 'Never, never ever' would he support Israel. He'd always support whoever Israel are against. Now, he has to readjust his love-hate relationship to soccer, and to politics.

Mahmoud has a dream – a dream fired by a single shot: Will Abbas's 90th minute equaliser provide equality beyond the 90 minutes?

Just by chance, by pure chance, I was at the National Stadium for the Abbas game. I wanted to sit with the Irish supporters. The police wouldn't let me into the Irish section. They told me, because 'I'm an Israeli', I couldn't. That's what they said. So there I was, drowning in a sea of blue-and-white Israeli scarves. All I could see was blue and white. I didn't have one of those T-shirts in the national colours which they'd handed out – they told me it was because I came late, not because I'm 'an Arab'. You can't imagine the sense of unity in that stand. It was so powerful. The sense of togetherness was so special. I began to feel change. You could really feel a kind of change in the air. I try to keep my distance: When they shout, 'Go Israel, go!' I yell, 'Abbas Suan, my Soul!'

Towards the end of the second half, Abbas comes on as a sub:

Go get 'em Abbas! To me, the whole crowd don't want him. So every time Abbas touches the ball, I yell: Aaaab-bas-Suan! Aaaab-bas-Suan! Each time Abbas touches the ball, I yell. Then, he scores! He's on his knees, bowing, offering a prayer. Suddenly, the whole stand falls on me, they're jumping on me, hugging me, kissing me, embracing me, lifting me on their shoulders, anointing me with a scarf. (This time, they didn't tell me it's because I'm an Arab.)

Suddenly, I feel I'm really part of these people, I'm one of them. On the way home, the excitement doesn't let up. I keep telling people: Say out loud, Abbas! Say Abbas! At every red light, I roll down the window, wave my blue-and-white scarf and shout to the driver alongside: Say Abbas, say Abbas, say it again! Get used to saying it. I stop next to one car flying the Israeli flag – he'd been to the match. I open the window. Say Abbas! I tell him. He says: Abbas! Again! I tell him. I want them to say Abbas! to get used to saying the name. Maybe that'll bring about the change – maybe? Who knows?

I drive back to Sakhnin with my blue-and-white scarf. In the morning, I wake up. I find the Israeli colours in bed sleeping peacefully alongside me. Believe me, I . . . I . . . I dunno what's happened to me! I see those colours in my bed, and I say to myself: How in God's name did this happen to me – a new definition of sleeping with the enemy?

Several of my friends advise me: This is simply no good, it's just not right. I try to convince myself that it *is* good – when a boy from my neighbourhood is hailed as 'Hero of Israel' – is that not good? My wife asks me: How far are you going, Mahmoud? What's happening to you? That far? But I try to convince myself that it *is* good. I see the headlines: they speak of 'Abbas Suan,

King of Israel' – a boy from my own neighbourhood . . . hailed as 'King of Israel'. Is that not good?

It takes a week for Mahmoud to find peace of mind. His conclusion: that the goal, and the Jewish reaction to it, are but a dream.

Then he revisits the National Stadium. Brutal reality back centre-pitch – a reality check of my dream: Sakhnin are again being hosted by Betar, this time in the league play-offs. Now, it's Betar who've been penalised for their rowdy fans. They must play two games away from home out of Jerusalem. Soon enough, the racist taunts by the unrepentant Betar crowd, a vigorous denial of acceptance of Abbas, darkens Mahmoud's dream. The dream is a nightmare: We believed that Abbas's goal would change their mentality, as it changed mine. But then they unfolded a giant banner, so large it covered the whole Betar stand – that's how much trouble they take to declare to the whole country, 'Abbas Suan, You Don't Represent Us'. How come they don't accept the player who brought such pride and hope to the whole nation, whom they crowned their hero, who made so many people feel so close to this country? Isn't that exactly what they say they want? But no, I'm listening in to their fans talking among themselves. One kid, he's about 16 or 17, he's banging a drum – he says, with disgust in his voice: Abbas Suan, a hero of Israel? What are you talking about – Abbas Suan is a hero of Palestine!

The day after the sordid Betar experience we get an urgent call from Sakhnin (Hey Mahmoud, what's up?). He's concerned. He hopes we haven't yet published his fervent feelings, his conversion, that tumbling soul-search in the wake of national euphoria, that embrace of the national minority by the majority:

All that I can now say is, Thank you, Betar fans! You've woken me from the dream, from the illusion. You've brought me back to the harsh reality which I thought had changed. The dream which I imagined might be a wonderful new reality turned into a nightmare. I prefer the nightmare, their dream. Their dream is that I accept their reality – the reality of not really being accepted, of not really being wanted in this country . . . unless, that is, we are prepared to play ball in the way that they want us to play ball. You can almost hear Taysir whispering to Mahmoud out loud behind his sunglasses: No luck, see, no luck!

But, in fact, Mahmoud's relieved that he's survived pseudo-acceptance: The Betar game made me realise why I wasn't happy with that dream of coexistence. My dream is a vision of acceptance as we are – not as they would like to fashion us. Soccer hasn't killed his politics – it's resuscitated them. The racist taunts are proof of that. In a paradoxical sort of way, his worst enemies have reassured him.

Forget Mahmoud's nightmare. What's kept the rest of the country awake ever since the Betar game was what happened while the national anthem was being played. The IFA leaves it to each club to decide whether to play *Hatikvah* before league games – Betar always choose to and it was their home game. Just as the national anthem began to play, the Betar fans got busy unfurling their giant anti-Abbas banner. That was what triggered the booing and jeering from the Sakhnin crowd that covered *Hatikvah* and so incensed the press. You definitely couldn't hear the anthem being sung way across on the Sakhnin far side of the pitch. That clamour is precisely what the critics of Sakhnin complain about. The hot game was actually completely pallid. It ended goalless. Yet there's talk of both sets of fans being hauled over the coals by the IFA disciplinary committee for 'uncivil conduct' during the pre-game proceedings.

Someone desperately needs to sober things up. Lachman, maybe? All season long, he's being anything but sober, parading Sakhnin as a trademark for excitement, proud that The Sons week by week, game by game, have been the talk of the country. Now he, too, is in a totally new league: I'm quietly trying to work the team into a nil-nil syndrome, to instill a sense of contentment that we do well by picking up one point at a time, one point each game, no more than that. That's the way to keep our heads up.

Hey, what's happened to Lachman? It's so not him to worship one point gained from a lousy draw, to forget about the two abandoned by not going whole hog for victory. Is the manager still managing or is he losing his touch? Or is he, like his nemesis Mahmoud, also learning to come to terms with reality?

Chapter 10

Understanding Each Other's Pain

'In the banality of our everyday lives'

UNDERSTANDING EACH other's pain, building bridges of conscience and of coexistence across the Jewish–Arab divide, was a critical part of the 'peace years' of the '90s.

Back then, for the first time, Israelis and Palestinians recognised each other's existence. In their quest to end their 100-year conflict, inevitably they were also drawn towards recognising the existence of the historic pain of the other – for Jewish Israelis, the Holocaust, *Shoah*; for Palestinians in general, and for Arab Israelis, the 1948 'great catastrophe', *Naqba*, the creation of Israel and the Palestinian exodus. Tentatively, each side began grappling with the validity, the sustainability of the other side's pain.

Then came the Palestinian uprising. It not only destroyed this willingness to reach out and to understand the other's pain, it's done far more damage: Each side has become numb, oblivious to the other's pain – each side left with the feeling that the only way to assuage its own pain is to inflict more pain on the other.

The same tenets of the equation, though less intense, are true for Jewish Israelis and Arab Israelis. The gap between their two pains is at its most stark during this season of remembrance, this untimely spring season of remembrance – of wars, of the Holocaust.

Sakhnin. 10am sharp. The siren blares out from 'Permanent Base 1003463', the army camp that overlooks the town. Slightly farther off, another echoes out from the Misgav Regional Council. A chilling sound. Monotonous, plaintive, unlike the up-and-down wail of war alarms that blare out at times of attack from across the borders – as when Saddam Hussein's Scuds rained down from Iraq during Gulf War I. The siren signals two minutes of silence. An elemental public moment: Holocaust Memorial Day – when Israel pays tribute to the memory of the six million Jews murdered by the Nazis. Most of the country grinds to a halt. Motorists and pedestrians stand sombrely at the road side.

Here, people go quietly about their business. Mundar Haleileh is at his desk as usual. His office is on Route 805, on the ground floor of the squat run-down municipality building. When he isn't speaking for Bnei Sakhnin, Mundar administers the local clinic of the National Health Fund. Through the window, the siren continues to wail away in the distance. Traffic continues to rumble down 805. Mundar listens in silence. Mundar has been to Auschwitz. Two years ago, the club spokesman cum master of philosophy was part of a delegation of Arab and Jewish Israelis who visited the death camp.

Whenever their team are on top and rival fans try to raise their own team with vocal support, the cry from the Sakhnin stand is 'Sit still, you maniacs!' Mundar's is another kind of 'sit still' approach: The proper response to the Holocaust is silence, deep silence. Every extra word reduces the pain of the Holocaust. Yesterday, I went onto the Internet. I went onto Google and I typed 'Holocaust'. From concentration camps to death camps – 2,000 camps in Germany, in Poland . . .

The distant siren dies away. There's a sudden stillness in the air. Mundar falls silent again, searching his memory: It's shocking. It leaves you paralysed – completely. You read, you recreate in your mind, you imagine. I visited Auschwitz, I recall the picture, the moment, and it's painful. To identify with pain is holy, perhaps, in the banality of our everyday lives.

He breaks off to type into his computer the record of a patient, a woman on crutches. She's come to get a referral to a Haifa hospital for a CT scan. Like an extra in a Bergman drama, she stands impassively waiting for Mundar to re-gather his thoughts: We all react differently. Some express anger, some express the evil in them, some express the good in them. So, if ever you're tempted to draw a parallel, don't – at least not out loud. It either hurts the pain of the Holocaust or you'll be misunderstood. But the moment that pain hits, and people identify, you get a feeling that humanity is triumphant, that humanity beats all. Identifying with pain can't be conditional; the moment it is, it loses credibility. There's another side, however. We're human beings after all and we have to relate to the situation in which we live, in which we have to live.

Is Mundar saying, 'Don't compare your own pain so as not to harm the relationship', or is it out of fear of . . . of intruding on the Holocaust itself, yes. First, not to impinge on the Holocaust.

That first! Second, you won't be understood, they won't understand you well. But, third, when all is said and done, if you don't draw a parallel, you come out sounding like a fool – a fool! You're pandering! Because, on one hand, you can't talk about the pain of the Holocaust. And, on the other, not talk about your own pain. There's a constant dualism between what your heart tells you and what your mind tells you. The heart says: It's pain. It's unfathomable. It's absurd. Your brain tells you: By God, there are other things!

Didn't Pascal say, 'The heart has reasons that reason cannot know'?

Again, I say, it's not to draw a parallel, but you can't be indifferent! The greatness of a human being is that even when you're part of a majority, you're able to feel the feelings of the minority, feel what the minority feels.

We, as Arabs, have to find the common ground, have to find a way to make heart and head meet. On one hand, to speak about the pain of the Holocaust, to identify with the Jewish people. But to know that we too have our pain – we too have our history.

Mundar's memory isn't everybody's. Not everyone wants to be in Auschwitz. Mundar's is still a lone voice.

Muhammad Mura is an educator from Kfar Qar'a in Wadi Ara, a couple of valleys down in the south of Galilee: The Jews did suffer in Europe. They suffered because they were a minority in Europe. So Jews should be sensitive to the predicament of minorities. They should really feel our suffering, feel for us.

Muhammad works under Zoheir Yehieh, the Kfar Qar'a mayor, a great fan of Sakhnin. Zoheir never misses a match. He was on both trips to Europe. He has a permanent pew alongside

Mayor Abu Shadi in the VIP stand. He's also charting his own line on the coexistence field and has set up an Arab-Jewish coexistence school, 'The Bi-lingual [Hebrew-Arabic] School in Kfar Qar'a'. There are a few other such bilingual Jewish-Arab schools elsewhere in the country, including one in Misgav to which some of the Sakhnin sons and daughters go. Zoheir's school is the only one in an Arab town. Noha Khatib is the Arab co-head of this unique school. She takes issue with her mayor's commitment to the Sakhnin way: Sure, Bnei Sakhnin is a challenge to us all, Jews and Arabs. But, let's not over-exaggerate the importance of soccer. The way I see it – our duty is to have our kids acknowledge the validity of the narrative of the kid next door. Soccer just can't do that on its own. As long as each side says: 'it's only mine, I don't play this game with anyone else', we'll be stuck forever.

That's the historic stand-off, the current stand-off: The Arabs of Israel are not formally required by the Jews of Israel to observe either Holocaust Memorial Day or Memorial Day for the Fallen in Battle which ushers in Independence Day. On neither day are they required to feel 'part of'. On both days, there's no required Jewish-Arab interaction of memory or mutual understanding of pain. But at the sound of the crackle of fireworks which marks the transition from Memorial Day to Independence Day, Arabs are asked to make a major shift: We don't ask that you identify with our fallen in battle, but we do insist that you respect the outcome of our victories in those battles (against your fathers). On both days, though, Arabs are asked to 'sit still, you maniacs!'

A football man displaced because of war between his peoples

In 1948, at the time of Israel's independence, Sakhnin was just a village of 2,850 people. The four mukhtars of the four big families – the Haleilehs, the Ghanaims, the Abu Rayas and the Zubeidats – took a critical decision, to remain come what may: We'll live here, we'll die here, they said. Only a handful left in 1948. They became refugees.

The focus is usually on the Palestinian refugees who are outside the country. But what about the 'internally displaced'? Now full Israeli citizens, but who, during the 1948 war, moved from their home village to elsewhere in the country. Sa'id Hamad Suan is one such 'internal refugee'.

As the father of Abbas, the man who, for a day at least, was the most famous Israeli – Jew or Arab – Sa'id Hamad's family have become overnight national celebrities. But on Independence Day, the Suans would rather be out of the public eye. It's a day off on which the Suan patriarch takes his family on a brief journey back to his home village, Murassass. It's a day 'when we won't be noticed'. He feels sure that Jewish Israelis will not look askance at his 'pilgrimage picnic'. That's because on Independence Day it's a hallowed tradition for Israelis to go out for a spring picnic.

Murassass is not on Israeli maps. What little remains of it is near Beit Shean – the sometime home of homeless Bnei Sakhnin. In 1948, when he was 11, Sa'id Hamad's parents moved to Sakhnin. He's come to terms with it. But now, six decades later, he still hasn't lost hope that Israel will eventually come to terms with his status, finally recognise its 'internal refugees'. The Suans wonder:

has their prodigal son, The Sons' legendary No.8 ('say Abbas!') really brought about a change in attitude?

Sa'id Hamad is no youngster, but he makes light work of clambering up on a tall kitchen stool to rummage through a big cardboard box at the back of a cupboard in his bedroom: See, this is a document from Mandatory Palestine – here's the government stamp, the *kushan* from the Property Rights Registry – in my father's name, Muhammad Dibb Abu Suan. Here's the name of our village – Murassass. With reverence, he repeats: Murassass, Murassass. And here's the date, 1/1/1927. I dunno who acquired the land since then, either Kibbutz Bet Hashita – sure, we're neighbours there in the valley, neighbours. Or, perhaps it was taken over by the State – I really don't know. Anyway, they took it over. 'State Property' they call it.

It was the time of the Turks. There was lots of land available. Whoever had 10 or 20 lira was able to buy a lot. And, if you did buy, you got a gift of some extra land. That's how our family got there. They distributed among themselves the land that they'd acquired. They built the village. Of all the villages in the area, Murassass had the most land. Some of his grandchildren wander in. They listen raptly to his story, watch wide-eyed, intrigued by their grandfather's pride, by the tears in his eyes: Do you know what it feels like when a man has his property taken from him? Sa'id Hamad is not bitter, just resigned. He deposits his precious document back at the top of the cupboard.

Abbas bursts in. All smiles and excitement – for the first time, he's decided to join the annual Independence Day outing: Dad and Issam – you go in one car, me and Uncle Dibb and Abdallah and Mohammed will go in my car. First time home in Murassass and he's already organising the transport arrangements to the picnic as he'd array his troops on the pitch. There's a buoyancy about the 'Hero of Israel'. He clearly doesn't remember how only a few months back, during Ramadan, he'd brushed it off, saying '1948 doesn't work for me.'

Uncle Dibb settles his black-and-white *keffiyeh* into the passenger seat in Abbas's Audi and turns on Koranic verses that are blaring out from the radio. He mumbles into his beard: *Yalla*, let's get moving already! Issam gets into the back of the other car. Sa'id Hamad is already in the front seat. With little Muhammad in her arms, Safa comes out to make sure of the picnic alibi, pops a thermos into the boot. She's swapped her white silk kerchief for a red-and-black balaclava with The Sons' stallion-and-ball.

You're sure it won't spill?

No, no you'll be fine.

I promise, I won't be late.

Safa smiles shyly. Abbas waves shyly.

C'mon, let's get moving already! *Yalla*.

Heading south-east through the choice farming areas of the Jezreel Valley, home to the first kibbutzim and Jewish collective farms that were settled in the early decades of the last century, a 45-minute drive to Murassass — a full half for Sa'id Hamad and Issam (my fourth eldest, fifth youngest) to play their hearts out.

When Abbas scored his goal against Ireland, we were so, so happy. I switched on to an Arab channel. They're saying: Abbas Suan, the Arab who saved Israel from itself. Dad gives a knowing chuckle and lights yet another cigarette. Issam isn't impressed.

They abandon us on the sidelines and still they say they want us to be 100 per cent part of the country — you go straight on through the junction, straight on. So they want us 100 per cent. Yet what they give us is no more than one per cent. It just doesn't add up. (Sometimes even history teachers like to make their most eloquent points through arithmetic.) Call this a democratic country, where things are all equal? Still, I'll never leave, never ever. Even if they were to offer me paradise, I'm staying put, right here. So why not let me feel, why not let the whole Arab community feel, that there's real equality. If that were to happen, I'm 100 per cent sure that everyone would be ready to commit themselves to everyone else. We'd all be ready to fight for the common good. Put yourself in my shoes, feel what I feel, is what I say. We're not going the right way. Something's gotta change.

It can't go on this way. It simply can't (yet another drag on yet another cigarette).

It all depends on them. It really all depends on them. It always depends on the strong. They're the ones who have to change. Whoever's the weak will always be worried, worried about how he looks to the strong. The weak always need reassurance: How do they view me? Have I done something wrong? Was I right? It's obvious – change must come from the strong. Turn left at the crossroad. Then, head north down a dirt track. There's no signpost.

Sa'id Hamad winds down the window. Nostalgia blows in: This is Murassass land. It used to be full of carob trees. We made sugar out of the fruit, red sugar. What a place, I'm telling you!

The training of Abbas

Reality hits.

Look, a new fence, they've made a new fence around the houses (or where they used to be). The kibbutz cattle were obviously getting out.

Dad strides impatiently alongside the long barbed-wire enclosure, murmuring half to himself, surveying the contours of his (lost) family property: They made a fence, they made a fence, they made a fence. That's the village there, and the cemetery alongside it.

Abbas is tending his feet. He's gingerly swapping his sandals for full gym shoes. You sure don't want to pick up an unnecessary injury clambering through the thorns. There's no point in emulating another hero, Achilles. Succumb to a sore heel and you risk your career as hero coming to an early end. He comes up alongside his father and the small family group who are peering over the low fence at the almost indistinguishable rubble of the long-gone houses. They gaze out down and across the peaceful valley. A cloudless sky has created a shadowy blue haze. The green alfalfa fields, and the yellow wheat beginning to sprout high in the early summer, mingle with patches of freshly ploughed earth. The good earth. Abbas is clearly affected by the moment. He's seeing it for the first time. He grows pensive. His handsome face looking out over the valley conjures up the vision of another hero of Israel – the young (though in Abbas's case, the beardless) Theodor Herzl, father of Zionism, immortalised in just such a pose, gazing out over a bridge in Basel in 1897 just before he'd compiled his treatise *Altneuland* (Old New Land) that advocated the creation of a Jewish state.

Where exactly is it, Dad? Where's the house?

Over there, near those trees.

Mohammed chuckles: Oh, you mean the land? Way down to there! He motions all the way off to the horizon trembling in the midday heat, Abbas giggles self-consciously. There's actually nothing to see but the beautiful view. A village with a view. But no village. Old Uncle Dibb spares Abbas's blushes. He kicks it off the line: 'Kumia, Yubla, Kafra . . .' a litany of names, the names of past villages, lost villages. He crouches low on his haunches, takes Mohammed's hand and pounds it to his heart: And Jaboul, and Kawkab el-Hawa, and Mtilli and Murassass.

Sa'id Hamad crumbles a tuft of the hard brown earth. Abbas brushes off a few stray thorns that have clung to his white three-quarter tracksuit bottoms. Sounds of crickets fill the air, rustling and scraping their wings in the long dry grass. Without warning, an opera singer searching for the perfect pitch, Uncle Dibb cups his hand to his ear. He sings from an epic Palestinian poem:

O, the bird which flies
On the wings of the air!
O, what has befallen my family
After the passion of separation?
Would that I were a tiny feather
Nestling in your wing.
Let us fly together
Back to the homeland.

Issam wipes an eye. Abbas, munching on a plum, has a shot at a quick translation: 'If only he could live here again . . .' In short, that's what it's about, remembering everything as it once was: He was born here, lived here, my uncle and my dad – both of them. From grandfather to his son, from father to his son, the message is handed down. That's our way. They teach us, we teach our kids – not to forget the land. We won't. The State took the land . . . (The State must return it, coaches Sa'id Hamad) . . . The State must return it. If Israel, our state – we're citizens after all –

believes in peace, in coexistence, if Israel believes in its own citizens, surely it's time for it to give back to its own citizens at least some of what's been taken over the years.

Heralded Abbas, emboldened Abbas, Murassass Abbas, Abbas prepared to talk politics for the first time. Not the politics of an Arab nationalist, mind you, insisting that Israel's Jewish character be done away. Abbas's appeal isn't about restoring the status quo ante 1948. Rather, they're about what's to be done now, 60 years into a whole new world, the world of the Jewish State, his state. It's the appeal of a citizen to fellow citizens, of citizen hero Abbas to his state – all because of one magical goal. With the goal – confident Abbas, immune to criticism.

If anyone's changed with the goal, it's Abbas himself.

A sober resignation settles over the little party of land pilgrims. They watch a black four-wheel drive packed with a family of picnickers sailing by, heading for an outing of their own in the hills. Through the jeep's trail of dust, they glimpse a small Israeli flag fluttering from the rear window. Abbas has a bitter-sweet insight: You see how it is? They've come to see their land – their land that's ours.

It may not have the makings of the 'Old New Land', but 'their land our land' is a jolly good formula on which to build real coexistence. Uncle Dibb has had enough of the hot sun: C'mon, let's get moving! *Yalla*, Abbas, get on with it. Let's go home.

Chapter 11

More Arab Than an Arab

Surviving self-doubt

NOT QUITE HOME, Abbas, not yet. First, an important stop at their 'home' ground in Nazareth. It's Sporting Club Ashdod again and it's bound to be a loaded match after that away game in the port town – that knock-out of Alain Massoudi, the libellous blaming of the victim for the ruckus, the pitch invasion by the Ashdod managers, Lachman taking the flak and nearly getting into a whole-scale melee with Mazen, the manager's 'I know best how to handle any outburst against my team' versus Mazen's 'promise to host' a *sulha* reconciliation ceremony at the Knesset.

Unlike real life where you may have only one chance to say sorry, or in the Jewish calendar which provides but a single 'day of reckoning' on the Day of Atonement – soccer allows at least two opportunities – home and away – and sometimes even three rounds in a season to come to terms, to settle scores with your enemy. Will today's game be a moment for Ashdod to say sorry, for Sakhnin to accept their atoning?

In the centre circle . . . see, hands are outstretched . . . they really do touch . . . the long awaited *sulha* . . .hearts beat fast . . . hearts united. But no, wait, they're withdrawing, each to their own side of the pitch. No *sulha* at all. All it is, is the usual soccer stuff before kick-off, the toss for sides and who kicks off. Sakhnin will be defending the falafel-stand end in the first half and attacking the Basilica-of-the-Annunciation goal.

Has Mazen wisened up? Has he backed off from soccer reconciliation? Is soccer stronger than reconciliation? In fact, there are no grudges. Mahmoud Ghalia, fresh from his personal saga – white nights, dreams and nightmares – is back on duty, recording the nitty-gritty of Sakhnin's triumphs and traumas: What happened in Ashdod was an ugly incident but it didn't run deep. We can forget how vicious it was. We Arabs tend to have short memories.

Well, today anyway, there'll be no outbursts among the fans. As a matter of fact, there aren't any Ashdod fans. Fear of reprisals or simply lack of commitment – it seems it's too far for them to trek all the way from near the border with Gaza to central Galilee. So Ashdod in Nazareth has fewer supporters than players on the pitch: three teenagers bedecked in yellow-and-red scarves. After they score their first and only goal, five more fans materialise. Obviously, they're no match for the 4,000 very vocal Sakhnin faithful. But thank goodness the *sulha* evangelists have been put in their place: *al-Ahli* journalist Mahmoud may be forgiving (or be ready to forget), but had there been a *sulha*, it would've taken the heat out of a very competitive game – The Sons and their fans would have been mollified by an overdose of hugging and kissing and weeping. With no *sulha*, Mazen's diplomatic skills are again called upon – this time, to quell rising tempers as the Ashdod players dare to match Sakhnin's tough tackling. His judicious handling of sticky situations has already earned him plenty of plaudits all around the country in the most unpredictable forums:

If Abu Mazen (the Palestinian President) had only half the touch of 'our Mazen', we'd have had peace with the Palestinians yesterday. [A junior official – Jewish – in the corridors of IFA power in the bowels of the National Stadium.]

I respect that Mazen – he's got class. He's the kind of guy you can rely on. If only they were all like him! [A diehard Betar fan in the Jerusalem *Sportoto* kiosk on Bethlehem Road run by former Betar legend Victor 'No.10' Levi.]

The real *sulha* happens during the game. Sakhnin's young midfielder Nidal Hudjeirat goes a long way towards removing the 'touch-tackling' stigma. They were still trailing to that early goal. Nidal is foraging on the edge of the Ashdod penalty area. An Ashdod defender – not clear who he is – is down injured, clearly in pain. Hudjeirat's got a real chance to score. Will he? Surely it must be a goal. But, no, he's turning away, he slides the ball out of play near the corner flag. Why? Let's look at the replay. Oh, he's chosen not to shoot so as to allow time for the physio to come on to treat Adir Tubul. That's the guy in pain who went down in that clash. That was noble, quite unusual too, a gentle clap on Hudjeirat's shoulder from referee Eran Frost for sportsmanship.

Later, Sakhnin celebrates a come-from-behind 2-1 victory expecting Lachman to spoil the party – 'why not 3-1?' – and criticising his young star for having been far too soft. Lachman spoils the expectation: They say we're not sporting. We may be strong and sharp, but we're as sporting as you can get. Has Lachman really gone soft this time, gone goody-goody? Not to worry — the man takes care not to be over-conciliatory. Out comes the old Lachman line: Don't underestimate the value of winning. Victory is a value supreme.

Victory supreme versus sportsmanship above all? Which is it, Eyal? Who's the true Lachman? Consistency isn't our forte, notes Mahmoud. American philosopher Ralph Waldo Emerson gets his name on the scoresheet: 'Consistency is the hobgoblin of small minds.' One thing you can certainly say about The Sons of Sakhnin — they're anything but small-minded.

A manager sent off

Bilal: Lachman was a good manager. Maybe he made a couple of mistakes. But, now that he's gone, we certainly shouldn't talk anything ill of him.

Tarek: Lachman's done his bit. Okay, well done. But, everyone has his limit.

Bilal: He reached his limit and . . .

Ahmad: He'll be back soon, you'll see, Bnei Sakhnin is his team . . .

Tarek: No, he won't, he won't be back. Anyone who fails can't come back.

Ahmad: What are you talking about — he didn't fail.

Tarek: You bet he did. Someone — the manager, the management, the players — we just gotta shake things up. One of that trio just had to go. So, Lachman was the bad genie. With him out of the bottle, let's see what happens . . .

Hard on the heels of that win over Ashdod, there've been four successive defeats. Mean old hubris standing around the corner has been lying in wait to club anyone guilty of succumbing to overconfidence. The Sons are beset by crisis. Round up the usual suspect: in soccer, a failing manager is no manager at all – he's got to go. Victory's supreme after all – Lachman would agree with that. And, when Sakhnin – town, club, supporters – believe that their existence – town, club, supporters – is in jeopardy, forget about coexistence between the manager and the club. The central suspect in the denouement is – who else – Alain Massoudi. Like father punishing recalcitrant son, Lachman refuses even to let him change into his training gear. In the Lachman school, that's what happens when you open up on your manager in a press interview – 'I'm at a loss to understand why I haven't been playing.' The midfielder is reduced to uncreative sulking in a corner of the dank changing room at the practice ground: *Il est dingue,* he's *dingue* – crazy, *complètement.* I don't know what he wants from me. Mad, he's mad. For three games in a row, Massoudi has not been in Lachman's starting line-up. Even as Sakhnin slid from defeat to defeat, he refused to bring him on.

The Massoudi–Lachman ruckus is driving Mazen *dingue –complètement* – I beg your pardon – it's Lachman who's creating the ruckus. Okay, I rely entirely on his judgement. He's got talent, I give you that. However, I paid a fortune for Massoudi, and I'm paying him a fortune every week – for what, to be sitting on the bench?

I beg *your* pardon – it's Massoudi creating the ruckus. Okay, he's got real talent, I give you that. But he's a lazy brat. I was warned by the Austrians at Sturm Graz when I went to negotiate his transfer. He's got skill, no doubt, but if you get a full season's play out of him – you're a true magician.

Who's boss? In this triangle, who will outlast whom?

It was just a matter of time: the running battle between manager and star, between manager and chairman, finally explodes during a 4-0 drubbing by Hapoel Haifa, the team at the very bottom of the league. The humiliation galls even more that Haifa are associated with The Sons' fondest memories – the glory of that magical night when they won the Cup which now seems so far away (and where is it anyway?). The club immediately adopts the traditional approach in the 'world-according-to-soccer' – they duly fire the manager. The word is put out: Eyal Lachman is no longer in a position to boost self-reliance or the team's dwindling self-confidence. Mazen is mean old hubris lying in wait to club down a manager guilty of succumbing to over-confidence. Premonition, perhaps, of another (Bermuda) triangle where the manager simply vanishes off the pitch – of Chelsea boss (Roman Abramovich) failing to convince manager (José Mourinho) to play star (Andrei Shevchenko) and we land up with a manager, Avram Grant, then the Israel manager, now a Chelsea discard too.

Lachman and Grant are good friends, battle-hardened brothers-in-arms, they like to boast. They regularly exchange notes. In contrast to Grant's turgid style of play with the national team, all season long, Lachman has paraded 'his' team as a trademark for excitement – proud that 'his' team, week by week, game by game, has been the talk of the country. But as the club sank deeper into crisis, Lachman moved into a more humble down-to-earth league, talked of working up a commitment to emulate Grant's penchant for draws, for last-gasp equalisers and so on. Self-awareness comes too late. After Friday afternoon's debacle in Haifa, Lachman's sent off. Mazen reasserts control over 'his' team. He puts paid to the Lachman way in Sakhnin.

Bilal: But, Lachman won us the Cup, didn't he?

Tarek: I still say – no way can he come back.

Ahmad: You'll see, next year he'll be back, to resume the job he began here.

Bilal: All I can tell you is that I love the guy.

Never 'Them' – always 'Us'

It's so nice that they say so. How decent people are up there. Lachman's still rooting all the way for the team that he'd led for nearly three seasons. He feels hurt. No doubt about that. But he isn't allowing any aggrieved feelings to get in the way of his true feelings for 'his' club: Actually, they're still with me all the time. I'm concerned that the team might yet, heaven forbid, go down. I really should put it all behind me because I can no longer influence things.

In his cosy living room in his comfortable apartment in the middling town of Hod HaSharon in the very middle of Israel, the fired manager sits under a massive framed print of Michelangelo's 'Creation of Man'. He delivers his 'Creation of Sakhnin' according to Eyal Lachman: They never talk of how their dedication makes it easier for them to survive in the league. You never hear them saying once we have our own home ground, you'll see we'll be unbeatable. When they talk of desperately needing a ground, they just want it as somewhere to be the hosts. They want to feel they exist by giving – not by getting from, but by giving to. Other people feel good when someone gives them something. These people, they want to give. That makes them feel they exist. Working folk, those who get up early every morning to their labour, hard-working people – they're the best. Salt of the earth, that's what they are. What are you having – tea, coffee, sugar, no sugar, milk, no milk? It's a whole new Lachman, out of his tracksuit, unexpectedly indecisive. While he talks, he opens a kitchen cupboard, immediately shuts it, opens another. He seems to be having a hard time doing two things at the same time, unable to replicate his touchline presence when he's controlling a game – in a single breath, bawling his men out and talking about the intrinsic nature of the game. Now he chaffs, I can't do two things at the same time, like enjoying a game and not winning.

Eyal brings over the tray of coffee and biscuits: By the way, it's exactly the same among us Jews – hard workers don't get the recognition they deserve. Sakhnin can only grow and flourish when they feel warmth and love, if they feel secure. Exactly like us. What they've got in Sakhnin is roots – roots that are strong, roots galore. When the chips are down, what counts is roots.

We grow up in this country convinced we've won all the wars. When we were kids and we heard Arabic in the street it was a bit scary. Hey, what's going on here? we'd wonder. He sets the tray down on the lounge table next to a pistol: It's my kid's gun, a toy. But once you grow up, you realise that's not the whole picture, that the other side is not exactly a dangerous enemy. I read many books about the British Mandate, the Zionist underground movements, the battles between them and the Arabs. No one's all good, or all bad – one side wholly good, the other wholly bad. That's why, when I arrived in Sakhnin, it rather suited me. I feel with those who suffer, with victims. I guess my approach suited them as well. You could call it a good match. All the time I was there, our goal was to survive, and to excite. We survived all right – until now – and we certainly created excitement. We always played tough, we never allowed ourselves to feel inferior. We never played as inferiors. We were always on the offensive – even if we weren't always right. That's what created the aura around the club.

He eats the chocolate biscuits he's been offering us, eats and talks, disproving his protest that he can't do two things at one and the same time: Will they survive? I ask myself. They'll be okay. Come the moment of truth, excellence will out. That's how it is with Israeli soccer in general. Just as when the country's under attack, the nation rallies, people unite. Perhaps now the players will take more responsibility. Personally, I'll feel a whole lot better if they don't go down. I won't have to face the fact that a whole life project has gone down the drain.

It's something I built with blood, sweat and tears. Now, it's been cut short – the values I've tried to instill, the kind of things you nurture so that a club reaps dividends some time in the distant future. But, truth be told, I should've been defeated a whole lot sooner.

The World According to Lachman, 0; The World According to Sakhnin, 1.

How many times before was my defeat on the cards. Yet we managed to survive, somehow. This time it was 'no go' for me. There's nothing I can do now. Every chairman of every football club in this country has one thing in common – they all prefer home-grown players. It's only natural. It keeps their wage bill down. It's the dream – to build a dream team from a nursery of local players. But the club didn't get the message. Every time I made demands of the foreign players, the management would go behind my back and comfort them. The worst possible thing they could've done. It undermines a team's very foundations. How they would console them! All that petting of the foreigners! No wonder when Saturday came, they simply weren't up to performing properly. I warned the management: This'll cost us dear. Still, they didn't understand. All they could see was a foreigner, a fragile guest moping on the sidelines – all because the manager had yelled a bit at the poor little darling. I didn't want them to be like every spoilt foreign player who comes to this country. They should've known – a foreigner who comes to this country is all too well aware that it's the end of his soccer road. They act accordingly. They play accordingly. They take things for granted. They train less hard. They put in less effort. For all that, they make the most money. I just couldn't afford that in Sakhnin. I brought over the best available. During the season, things began to go wrong.

But what's the main complaint that the management has levelled against Eyal Lachman? That he relied too much on home-grown players, that he was too tough on the foreigners. What exactly does too tough boil down to?

Any foreigner – if you don't make demands, he gives you nothing. He respects only those who make demands, not those who kowtow. All week long, I have to make demands in order to get the results on Saturday. If I'd have had my way, there's not a shred of a doubt that, at the end of the day, they would've become total players.

Hang on a sec, just let me get rid of this call: Hullo, who's that? Oh, Avram . . . thanks for calling . . . Thanks Avram . . . thanks again Avram . . . Not a truer word, Avram . . . Thanks again for calling Avram . . . stay in touch . . . be in touch . . . Bye Avram.

That was Avram.

'Avram', we've gathered, is Avram Grant.

Since I'm home, all the guys are phoning. But, guess who's calling most – the foreign players. They've come down from the giddy heights of Europe. They know precisely what it means to have a manager who makes demands of them. But they were given the chance to give less, and look at the results. It's human nature – give as little as possible, take as much as possible. Take Ernest Etchi, he's almost 30, he won't be going back to play in Europe any more. Take Agoye Olomide, he's already 30. He hasn't had a club in Europe for three years. They're here to make a living. Great, let them make their living. But you have to give more than the others. After all, you're making $4,000 a month whereas a Sakhnin kid makes only $500. Should he run faster than you? Not on my watch.

If the club management has decided that this is why their manager is no good, well then . . . Lachman sips his tea, munches another biscuit: I can assure you I can also be gentle – when I have to – certainly, with my home boys. And, boy, how they've flourished – Abbas is the perfect example. And Ahmad (Kassoum) and Nidal (Hudjeirat) and Abed (Rabbah) and all the others. They'll mature into really talented players but only if they get plenty of warmth and love. You've got to be nurturing their self-confidence all the time. I like pep talks – that helps – but sometimes anti-pep talks help too, the kind of talk you need to calm things down. When do you do that? When your team falls into a routine and needs desperately to be shaken up. Then you say: Guys, I saw you this week, I saw how fired up you are before the game. Or, the opposite, when you realise that your team is inspired, like before a critical game with Betar: Guys, I'm really happy to see how calm you are, how cool and collected you appear to be.

You see where it's got you, Eyal, pretty ironic, all this affirmative action of yours for home-grown players. And, where do you land up – hustled off the ball.

But it was the right thing to do. It's just that I got undone by an opposite worldview. Some talk about the need to understand 'Arab mentality'. It's just not right to talk like that. Talking about 'mentality' is never right. Aren't there mentalities everywhere? You've got to steer clear of stereotypes. But what really gets my goat is wasted opportunity. Many leading Arabs within their community simply can't believe that their own Sons have it in them to survive the big time. What the club really needs is to belong to all the Arabs of Israel – I mean really belong. That's why it bothered me so much to see players like Ahmad and Nidal being treated like outsiders by their own community. As if they don't belong to Sakhnin just because they weren't born there. It's such a small place. They can survive. They will survive – if only they get the total support of all of Israel's million-plus Arabs. But whatever happens, I'm confident that so long as they remain just the way they are in Sakhnin – good-hearted, enthusiastic, willing to give absolutely their all – they'll be fine. They're not going to fade easily – so long as they don't change.

I'll tell you what does worry me, though – that some Jews will try to exploit my dismissal to counterattack the way Jews and Arabs have come together in Sakhnin. You could say there are really two camps within the Jewish camp: the opponents have become fiercer, but the silent majority – those who weren't really aware, who didn't have an opinion, who didn't know anything really about Arabs – have begun to understand and even to identify with the challenge which Sakhnin is putting out. Some have even become fervent supporters. Sure, those who never liked Sakhnin anyway are telling me: We told you so. You shouldn't have believed in them. But anyone with that line is just trying to make mischief. By the way, I don't rule out that it was a smart move by Mazen. Maybe it's a good move. But one thing I can tell the 'we-told-you-so' mob: I wasn't fired because I'm a Jew.

Maybe not 'because I'm a Jew', but perhaps because I've been more Arab than an Arab. The wicked unexpected cross comes from the corner of his mind. For once, Eyal is unwilling to meet a difficult cross head-on. He glances it harmlessly over the crossbar: Know what? Let's be positive: I've completed my work with my Sons still in the top league. That's success in itself – to have survived in a strong league, having coached them for 90 games without a single home game!

Actually, Lachman has no cause to be so hard on himself just because, for once, he's held back on a header. Throughout the season, on many an occasion, his forthright no-nonsense approach has enabled him to find the back of the net. An honesty which led him to take for granted – at the risk of being at odds with most fellow Jewish Israelis – that he and the other Jewish Sons of Sakhnin are playing for their Arab club to win and don't just see themselves simply playing for coexistence with the petty goal of getting a draw. Lachman's real strength lay in understanding that The Sons are an Arab team, an Arab–Jewish team only once its identity as an Arab team has first been accepted. When the majority accepts to play ball with the minority, it must sometimes accept a minor role – on the minority team's bench. Lachman saw that crystal clear.

Bilal: I told you I love the guy – he made them play on our pitch.

Tarek: All right, his tactics were fine. But, I still have my reservations about his dirty play.

Ahmad: The real problem is – look where he's left us: Cup holders battling for survival.

Wurrod Miari, the woman who talked to the Palestinian supporters in Tirana, rushes out of her third grade classroom to defend Lachman: His failures are not his, they're Sakhnin's failures. We have to acknowledge our mistakes, understand why we failed. The players, the manager, the management have all lost – we've all lost together, not Lachman alone. And, now we've lost Lachman! After he scored such handsome goals for the town, the way he spoke for the town. 'We in Sakhnin', he'd say – not 'them in Sakhnin'. He'd never talk about us, he talked with us. He never talked about 'yours', always about 'ours'. Always 'us', 'we', 'we will', 'we will win'. I'm so sad he's gone. He spoke his heart, he understood our heart. He became so much part of Sakhnin. How can you cut out your own heart?

Chapter 12

Rejoice – it's Lawn Day

Dawn, Lawn Day

A PINK DAWN BREAKS over Sakhnin. Shreds of dark black clouds are gathering menacingly off to the north-east. But on a day as holy as this, shadows will know their place: They'll not trouble the faithful. Rain is always blessed in a parched land. But today, Sakhnin wants another kind of kindness from the heavens: Clear skies and cooling winds. An emerald light shines out from Palestine Mosque in the West Stand, a lighthouse in the mist, a bright beacon against the pink-black morning sky. It's Friday, but few will choose to rest long this Sabbath morn. Everyone will soon want to look in on the action.

For the umpteenth time, Abdullah Ghanaim looks at his watch. 5.14am. I think I can get going now; they must have gotten going already. He turns over yet again. Finally, impatience gets the better of him. He tosses off the shiny red quilt that serves as his bedcover. No wonder he's been awake for hours. It's not just the excitement. The plastic quilt is hardly calculated to keep out the sharp chill of the spring morning. But Abdullah feels comforted under the Hebrew slogan that adorns the quilt: 'Sakhnin Sets a Decent Standard'. He doesn't need long to get going. Abdullah's already fully decked-out in his Sakhnin togs. While awaiting the appointed hour, he's been limbering up under the quilt of model behaviour, stretching and turning like a player priming himself for a Cup Final. All he needs is to don his red-and-white scarf and to adorn his neck with the stallion-on-the-ball charm. No coffee, no loo, no nothing. Just a last fond look at the Turkish-style minaret of Palestine Mosque that sits slap opposite the Ghanaims' lounge window. It overwhelms the view: 'Ours' and, at last, let's get going. 5.19am.

Rejoice! It's Lawn Day! Wake up! Wake Up! Lawn Day is here! Hey, everybody up! Abdullah's impatience is matched by his speed. It's hard to keep pace with the rollicking gay stride: Up, up, rejoice! It's Lawn Day!

Abdullah makes a quick calculation: From home, by foot, I'll be there in just five minutes, maybe seven, if I bump into somebody. By 5.26am at the latest, I'll be there. God, it's great. Dreamily, he keeps his mission going: Morning, how are you doing? Morning, morning, *yalla* let's get moving already. A real sleepwalker, Abdullah. Not a dog stirring. He's unfazed. No work today, it's a celebration, a real holiday – *'Id e-Deshe, 'Id e-Deshe*, a mix of Arabic and Hebrew for the national holiday he's just created – Lawn Day, the Festival of the Lawn. The town sleepwalker is now a preacher calling the invisible faithful to join him in giving thanks. A soft chant – *'Id e-Deshe, 'Id e-Deshe* – Abdullah's communes with his private joy, dreaming in his sleep.

Rejoice – it's Lawn Day

5.24am. Five minutes, spot on! Abdullah reaches the old iron gate on the eastern side of the stadium – the stadium he's busy building with his own two hands, the stadium he deconstructed with his jackhammer, the stadium he's now reconstructing with his trowel and mortar. For a brief second, the No.1 Fan of The Sons of Sakhnin hesitates: Dare he enter? A mini-tractor bundles by. He takes the plunge: We'll play here. Where does he go next, what does he touch next? *'Id e-Deshe* – the day that heralds the first tufts of grass in the revamped stadium. Abdullah takes another tentative step – wanting to tread on the tentative new grass, wary of doing it damage. Another small step. Gently, he strokes the clump of brown turf that's just been laid: I can't believe it – grass!

Gingerly, Abdullah makes his way around the touchline to his stands. He wants a bird's eye view, the fan's view: Soon we're going to play here – on our own grass. Well before dawn broke, even before Abdullah got going, the bevy of grass-seeders had invaded, sprouting from the well-watered soil. Armed with rakes, they took their bundles of turf in big hessian bags tied around the waist and ever since they've been spreading the clods of pre-prepared turf according to a meticulous plan. Intently, Abdullah watches the workers go about their business. They're airily suspended above the new clods of grass for fear of harming it: Once the clods are scattered, they shouldn't be trodden upon. But, within hours, Sakhnin's holy ground will begin to wear green. For Abdullah, it's already playing in brilliant technicolour, the green meshing with Sakhnin's red-and-white. Ah, there's some Betar black-and-yellow. No worry, those visiting colours won't make much impact on the complexion of this ground. A rosy dawn has settled on Sakhnin forever.

185

The gloomy clouds are fast dissipating. The sun peeks out at last, revealing three others perched high up on the concrete stands. The Three Wise Fans here to greet the newborn are already on duty to witness the day for the benefit of future generations and to solemnly pronounce their findings:

Bilal: The moment we've been waiting for.

Ahmad: Magical day, pure magic.

Tarek: I don't celebrate till I see a win on this ground.

Bilal: With a home ground like this, how can you doubt we'll win?

Tarek: I got to see results first.

Ahmad: Put a sock in it, Tarek. Don't spoil the party. Look at this lawn work – isn't it great?

Bilal: Right, this is top drawer, first class, first team, first town grass.

Tarek: I'll buy that the day the stadium's completed. We've had too many setbacks.

Ahmad: Grumble on, I can't wait till the first home game.

Bilal: Then, even Tarek will have to admit we'll be important.

Ahmad: Then, we'll get the recognition we deserve.

Sign of recognition: The bevy of TV cameras that've rolled in to record the historic day. There's Mazen accompanied by his elderly father Abu Mazen, and Abu Shadi, and Abu Majdi, Sakhnin's legendary headmaster, and journalist Mahmoud, mayor's spokesman Ghazal and club spokesman Mundar – the dads of Sakhnin are here to provide for their Sons. Dressed in all their finery. As one does on a holy day: *chag sameach*, *'id sa'id* – happy holiday. There are more than the customary three-cheek-kiss greetings. An extra one for good measure. For victory. But, time first to indulge in the hot coffee and *burekas* which Mazen has thoughtfully laid on to sustain the early morning revel. Even the cameras join in. The dads pose, holding up clumps of turf like a victorious XI holding up the trophy. The cameras whirr.

The chairman's prepared to let his usually circumspect self remain in bed. He's more candid than ever: The cameras flash, blinding the fast-rising sun. Solemnly, Mazen declares: You stand here on this patch of lawn and you know it's your land. You're here to serve the people up there in the stands. You know that they're your people, that they love you, that they support you. It strengthens us. It's worth years into the future. At last, we're on firm ground. From here, we look forward. Yet we don't forget for a second that we're a minority here. When a minority doesn't get the rights due it, then your first obligation is to preserve what you have. My team is in the top division. I have to keep it there, so as to be able to tell everyone what's still lacking, what still hurts. And to be heard. Today, we say a dream comes true. We celebrate. But still, we don't lose sight of what's lacking – and how great still is the pain.

Once, well before The Sons became a challenge, we interviewed Ariel Sharon at his Sycamore Ranch in the Negev desert. In his cowshed, symbol of his attachment to his ranch, to the land, to the country he saw as his ranch, we ask his view on the rights of Arab Israelis and on their place on this pitch. He comes up with this intriguing formula: They have all rights *in* the land, no rights *to* the land. This is now an accepted chant among many Israeli Jews.

Day after day, month after month, game by game, Sakhnin's relations with the State of Israel are tested against that formula. Do 'rights *in*' (Jews AND Arabs) versus 'rights *to*' (Jews ONLY) stop at the touchlines of this 113.75 x 73.66 yard strip

(105 x 68 metres) of home land – the size of the new home pitch
– which Ariel Sharon is himself helping create?

Abu Majdi, the headmaster, marks Sharon closely: If there are
no rights to the land, then no rights in the world are worth
anything. If you have no right to your land, which you never
took from anyone, never stole from anyone, then no rights have
any value at all. The land is the basis, the land is the right! Look
at all the area they've confiscated. For 'public benefit', they say.
Are we not the public too?

Abu Shadi puts his arm around him: We have to accept that
land's taken 'for public needs, for national needs'. We don't
challenge that. The land won't be returned, I recognise that. But
why shouldn't the land on which they've built the army base, and
that of the industrial district, be rezoned again? Let it revert to
our jurisdiction. Honestly, I don't see why we're excluded from
the Misgav Industrial Park. Why can't we share it with them? By
sharing, Sakhnin would benefit from the municipal taxes from
the army installations and the industrial park. It'd usher in a
whole new era in relations with the state. And with our Jewish
neighbours too.

The mayor's land strategy is truly revolutionary. It's a whole
different kettle of fish compared to the two-way finger-pointing
that's standard fare in the political discourse, especially since the
usual strident demands of Arab politicians have rarely got any
land returned. Suddenly, you realise that what Sakhnin is
devising is actually a very deft way to beat the state's offside land
trap. And all from a tiny little stadium . . .

Koby Mamo is here for the day. He's one of the Jewish brigade
of grass sprinklers from Tirat Ha-Carmel. Just out of the army,
Koby's regular job is security on the railways. A big burly fellow.

Swarthy. And, a kind heart. He can certainly do two things at the same time – he talks as he sows: It's a privilege to be here – I loved Abbas's goal. 'Hero of Israel,' they call him in the papers. Not quite 'hero'. All right, you can even say 'hero'. But I sure liked how he did it, the way he was happy after the goal. And his shot – boy, it was his whole heart. He didn't care about anything – religion, Arabs, Jews, land, politics. I'm really proud of him. I'm working here for them, but honestly that's not why I'm for them. Abbas did something grand. He did it with all his heart. He really didn't deserve what the Betar Jerusalem fans did to him, booing him when he was playing for Israel and saying 'you don't represent us'. Honestly, Sakhnin deserves better. They won our Cup, didn't they? They lifted the Cup and they deserve to be in the league, don't they? Especially since Abbas saved – you can really say 'saved' – Israel. At the last minute, a goal – heart and soul. That's what I believe. I hope with all my heart they stay up. But you've also got to say that what they did to Lachman wasn't nice. Simply, not nice. How does the saying go – you've got to stick together, in fire and in water. Haven't you?

Chapter 13

Survival

'Bnei Sakhnin Wake Up!'

POWERFUL SHOT WRECKS the back of the net – grey window shutters, actually. The ball rebounds and careens through the entrance of the courtyard. *Dir balkum!* Watch out! The ball has landed out into the 805, the busy touchline of the improvised concrete pitch. An errant ball, errant dreams. Before any of the red No. 8s (aged 3 to 12) can rush out into the road, even before a teenage No. 8 who's wandered in from school can come to the rescue and retrieve the ball, it's intercepted by a heavy duty truck racing past. The ball is squashed. Sakhnin's increasingly a place of punctured soccer balls, of deflated dreams.

No. 8 is the courtyard's most famous son, Abbas. The Suan family courtyard embraces a clutch of homes in which the brothers and their families live, the sons and daughters-in-law and grandchildren of the two patriarch brothers, Said Hamad Suan and

Dibb Badarneh. An engaging place: Kids exchange bikes and tricycles as comfortably as they exchange passes on the compact pitch which doubles as communal living space. A brand new leather ball is quickly rolled out from one of the houses onto the penalty spot. The game resumes. It's all about trying to emulate the most famous shot in town: long live heroic last-gasp equalisers!

Deflated dreams are all too routine this season. Emotions have been fluctuating wildly from euphoric highs, like *the* goal, to abysmal lows, like the surrender of the State Cup last weekend when another last-minute goal, by another underdog team, Hakoach Ramat Gan, bundled The Sons out of this year's Cup in the fourth round. The Cup has been taken, the Cup has to be returned. But where's . . . Just don't, don't ask.

Still, there's compensation for losing the Cup: at the start of next season, there'll be no return to Europe, no need to pencil in exciting journeys to Newcastle, or even Albania. All season long, 'We have a dream', and 'We shall survive' have been the mantras, *Hamsa!*, the sign of the hand invoked to ward off collective disaster. Now, all of a sudden, uncertainty stalks the pitch: Sakhnin are not in such great shakes in the league either.

Self-doubt is challenging self-reliance. Confidence is rock-bottom. 'Can we survive?' is the new state of mind. 'We shall overcome' has become 'Shall we overcome?'

'Bnei Sakhnin Wake Up!'

Someone has scrawled the wake-up call graffiti (in Hebrew) under the picture of a guy in an early-morning stretch in an Arabic advert for Arabic coffee (of an Israeli firm) on the billboard that greets you on arrival as you pass the army base at the entrance to town. The place may be incongruous but the injunction couldn't be more opportune. Mazen has felt compelled to pronounce that after three games in charge, Lachman's replacement, Momi Za'afaran, will stay with the club 'through the rest of the season'. Za'afaran, the now disgruntled faithful recall, was once with The Sons when they were in the third division.

Tonight, Za'afaran knows he must win if he wants to keep his promise to Mazen that he'll 'correct' the Lachman legacy. Thus far, it hasn't gone all that well for the new manager. His legacy so far is one victory, two defeats. It's a dog-fight at the bottom with three teams struggling to extricate themselves from the relegation zone. One of the three will join Kfar Saba – they're already doomed. If they beat Hapoel Tel Aviv away this evening, they'll be doing themselves a double favour. The Tel Avivians are also in danger. They, too, desperately need to win.

What do we have other than survival? Well, you can also have superstition, and God, and conspiracy, or just plain old good luck. Which of that quartet now sits on top of the league for those at the bottom of the league? The argument rages. It may never be settled. There are places, they say, where soccer is religion. At Sons' games, you hear the chants of '*Allahu akbar*' ('God is greatest' – in Arabic) and '*Yesh Elohim*' ('There is God' – in Hebrew) as often as '*Yalla* Sakhnin, *yalla*' ('Go Sakhnin, go' – in Arabic and Hebrew). But, don't misunderstand soccer-crazy Sakhnin. It's not one of those 'soccer is religion' places. There's a clear separation between church and town. Religion stands apart, above. Soccer is not religion, it's politics. God may be very much in their game, but the boundaries of soccer and religion are retained. You never know the result of a game, but you never doubt the result of your faith: God is always there – Mundar Haleileh speaks for the club – helping us when we win, testing our faith when we lose.

Lose! God forbid! Actually – nearly always in recent weeks. As things have gone from bad to worse, and worse still, the fans in Sakhnin are beginning to subscribe seriously to the notion that their very existence is in jeopardy simply because their soccer future is under real threat. It's fertile ground for one of the quartet – superstition, conspiracy, luck, God – to come into play. Or for all four to come into play?

The Sons' fans and the Hapoel Tel Aviv fans gather for their classic six-pointer clash. Conspiracy is all the rage. Outside the stadium – strategically parked near the ticket offices – a mini-van of *Sportoto*, the state-run pools organisation. It's not the opportunity of a last-minute pre-kick-off wager that creates a run on the van. The attraction is the live TV broadcast which the pools clerks in the van are watching. Another critical match in the relegation battle kicked off an hour earlier than our game and Taysir and his built-in transistor radio haven't yet arrived to update the score. Hapoel Beersheba are hosting Betar Jerusalem. Betar are safe in the middle of the league, Beersheba are fellow strugglers with The Sons. It's not clear where Beersheba's ideological inclinations lie – with Betar, or with Sakhnin and Hapoel Tel Aviv who both regard Betar as 'the national enemy'. And Betar, who hate both The Sons and Tel Aviv – how do they shape up in this mix? The Sakhnin fans are also in turmoil. For once, they don't know what they want.

'More *Toto*, more luck,' the jingle blares out.

Tarek: Luck? Luck's nothing to do with it.

Ahmad: Betar are going to get one over us and Tel Aviv at the same time. I'm worried.

Tarek: It's a conspiracy.

Bilal: They don't want us in the league?

Ahmad: They'll do everything, anything and everything, to send us down.

Bilal: You bet. They'll let Beersheba win just to get back at us.

Tarek: Why not have a bet on it?

Bilal: Great idea, let's bet on Betar to win!

Ahmad: Did you hear what you just said?

Tarek: You want Betar to win!

Bilal: That's not what I meant . . .

Tarek: So you don't want Betar to win.

Ahmad: So you want us to go down.

Bilal: C'mon, that's not what I meant either. You know what I . . .

Tarek: Forget it, look Beersheba have just gone one up.

Ahmad: Beersheba are safe.

Bilal: And, we're lost.

Gloomily, they troop off to watch Sakhnin take fate into their own legs. Gloomily? Did you hear what you just said – is self-reliance gloom? Who wants to rely on Betar to save them? Even in survival, you've got to stick to your principles, right?

They're out of earshot when a cheer goes up from the van. Conspiracy is laid to rest. Betar equalise. In fact, they go on to win 3-1. Imagine, Sakhnin delighted with Betar winning. God Forbid! Now that's the conspiracy – somebody must have set us up. Forget it, we're on our own. Nobody's going to do us any favours. Win, we survive. Lose, we agonise for another week.

Away from petty calculations – who gets the thumbs up, who gets the thumbs down – in the lion's den, there's an island of tranquility. All is quiet in The Sons' dressing room. Everything's under control. Everyone's cool:

Meir Cohen: Close the door, you idiot!

Eid Yassin: Who's next for a rub?

Massoudi: *Moi*, Alain.

Eid: How long have I got still? I've still got bandages to do.

Massoudi: Jamal, move out the way.

Jamal Ghnaim: *Mon chéri*, my beloved father of an ass!

Massoudi: Watch your tongue, please.

Jamal Ghnaim: You, you go screw your mother.

Massoudi: Hey, language, language.

Jamal Ghnaim: I'll forgive you everything, *mon amour* – just score tonight, you French bastard.

Massoudi: These people, this team, they're crazy: *Complètement dingues*!

Eid: Will someone please take notice of me. Will anyone please tell me how long I've got still?

Meir Cohen: Move on already, Massoudi. I need to get a rub too.

Jamal Ghnaim: Goalies, what do goalies need a rub for?

The stadium's a sea of red . . . on the Tel Aviv side. Red's the traditional Hapoel colour. It's Hapoel Bnei Sakhnin United's colour as well. But, scarves apart, most Sakhnin fans don't wear the traditional soccer jerseys of their team. Is it the expense? Or just that identification with the club is so much deeper than skin deep? Or is it that they don't want anyone mistaking their absolute commitment for the automatic behaviour of the herd?

An enormous roar greets Momi Za'afaran's chosen XI. They're out for the pre-game warm-up. Ab-bas Su-an! Ab-bas Su-an! – a familiar bellow from behind the backs of the standing ovation. Taysir has arrived. From his Bluetooth radio implant, he updates those who missed the game at the *Sportoto* van: Betar 3,

Beersheba 1 – who'd have believed it? I was sure they'd let Beersheba win just to screw us.

There's only one Abbas. Taysir leads the chant for the hero. His toothy smile confirms he's a one-love, one-family fan: Ab-bas Su-an! Ab-bas Su-an! Pigalle descends on the turf. Momi's the ballet master: High kick, quick sprints, left-to-right, right-to-left, *pas de deux*, *chassé-croisé*, *tendu*, knees-up, bums out, turns around, spin on the spot. The Sons strut their Folies-Bergères stuff in perfect synchronisation with the singing of the Tel Aviv crowd whose songs way outdo anything Sakhnin can produce. No one in their crowd, though, can match the beat of Sakhnin's very own follies – courtesy of Gumbul and his Trio. Once they get going on their drums, it's 'Welcome to Hell'. We'll show you who's at home here. Welcome home Tel Aviv, this is your hell.

Like Taysir, Aeilin Zuabi and Jamal Easa'a are fervent outside supporters. Aeilin is from Tamra, west of Sakhnin. Jamal is from Baq'a al-Gharbiya, south of Sakhnin. Salt-of-the-earth supporters. They revel in every victory. These days, they mostly pain in defeat. They approach Mazen standing near the tunnel. Mazen approaches a cop. It's Shimon:

Shimon, my brother, these fellows believe in salt. Can you allow them on?

Sure, if that's what you want, Mazen, my-brother-the-policeman tells him.

Thanks my brother. They believe in these things. What can I do? I have to respect their beliefs. It's a delicate two-step minuet: tolerating superstition and pandering to sensibilities. Whatever, Mazen's intervention does the trick. He wins special dispensation from Shimon-my-brother and Aeilin and Jamal are able to get onto the pitch to have the opportunity to spread their (Saudi) crumbs and their (Israeli) Dead Sea salt in the goalmouths.

Where are you putting the salt?

I put it on the goal line, in both goalmouths. Sakhnin's balls go in. But in Sakhnin's goal, the ball stays out – you understand. It's luck.

Shimon-the-Policeman nods politely.

Aeilin and Jamal spread their charms:

This is pita bread from Saudi Arabia. It's special stuff to break the jinx. Sakhnin will win, God willing, we'll stay in the league. Now, I'm laying it . . .

Shimon-the-Policeman nods politely.

Sakhnin plays good soccer. But, luck hasn't helped us. Today, we will break the jinx. And, we will stay up.

Another polite police nod.

They run from the *Toto* advert end to the Lotto advert end. Luck is all around. But Aeilin and Jamal are taking no chances that the *nakhss* (bad omen) might just survive their onslaught. They spread their bread and salt liberally on both goal lines to choke the jinx.

Aeilin has a back-up plan. He intends that the evil eye won't have even a ghost of a chance. On the edge of the penalty area, goalkeeper Meir Cohen's warming up with the goalkeeping coach. He tumbles, grabs crosses, clutches high balls, rolls, and rolls again. He's getting his eye in, his eye-hand coordination perfect. He trusts nothing to fortune.

Aeilin materialises miraculously with his plastic bag.

Shimon-the-Policeman is agitated.

Don't be afraid. Just keep practising.

I'm not afraid.

This is special stuff from Saudi Arabia.

A rain of good omen flakes flutter over the goalie's head. They settle. He looks like he's just contracted a bad bout of dandruff.

Great. Enough.

It'll give you confidence.

I am confident.

Inshallah, God willing, victory is ours, we stay up.

OK, thanks, now let me warm up.

The goalie brushes the dandruff off the back of his head and shoulders.

Back with Mazen, Shimon-my-brother recovers his composure: Good luck, Mazen. Your crowd looks happy. But Mazen's already heading for the dressing room to tend to preparations before kick-off: I only hope that at the end of the game they'll still be as happy, is his parting premonition.

Happy? After almost 90 minutes of non-stop jumping up and down on the edge of his blue plastic seat, Abdullah's still as taut as a drum, taut as Gumbul's hands beating his *darbuka*. Up and down, up and down, living every attacking Sakhnin chance, dying every near Tel Aviv miss, keeping his balance miraculously. It's an even game, a classic relegation tussle. Right up until 10 minutes before the final whistle: then Abdullah collapses in a heap and vanishes behind the blue plastic. A deflated balloon. No Abdullah re-bound this time. What a poor pass, what a fatal mistake, it's snapped up on the edge of the Sakhnin six-yard box, rammed home without mercy. A real six-point goal. Hapoel Tel Aviv 1, Bnei Sakhnin 0. Abdullah pops up from behind the plastic, lifts his head briefly with his hands – a major effort: Abbas, oh shit, Abbas. Abbas – that poor pass, it just had to be Abbas.

A pierced drum, Gumbul tosses his *darbuka* aside. It utters a broken twang, surprised at the unexpected ill-treatment by its devoted master. Gumbul recants. He re-gathers the drum, turns it upside-down and sits disconsolately on top of it. He's inconsolable. He turns up to the VIP box at the top of the stand. Mazen's face is sullen, mortally pale. Gumbul screams at the chairman and the other Sakhnin bigwigs behind the glass. With his drum in enforced silence, Gumbul is not one to mince words. He shakes his fist: You pigs! You sons of bitches! You screwed us! There are people who died 'cause of you, pigs! Son of a bitch! Why don't you sell Abbas to Betar – for free? It's all over. It's all over.

Not all over yet, but jolly nearly. Gumbul picks up his drum. In commiseration, it keeps its peace: I'm going. Nidal Hudjeirat has just been substituted. On the side of the pitch, he almost does himself serious injury kicking hard at an irrigation tap. The whistle sounds. Abbas comes off grim-faced, his head high. A bunch of fans pounce on him, tearing to get at him through the perimeter fence. The thumb-downers claw at the fence, yelling, cursing, charging his heart is no longer in the club – you maniac, you only want to shine in the national team. The word 'traitor' isn't heard. The thought's definitely in the air. The fence holds. Only just. The captain is no shirker. His poise is of Coriolanus, Shakespeare's general who keeps the barbarian hordes at bay at the gates of Rome only to find the once-adoring plebeians turning on him, accusing him of haughtiness. No one can ever accuse Abbas of being haughty, but he stands his ground. He wants to argue with the taunts. He puts his finger to his lips, angrily intimates that the thumb-downers should shut up, or else. The cursers are not stilled. Shimon-the-Policeman coaxes Abbas away: *Yalla* Abbas, come on. Nidal pushes him gently to the tunnel, wanting to avoid a direct show-down with the mob. The fallen hero wants to have it out with them. Reluctantly, he consents to be shepherded into the dressing room. The abusers rant into the fast-emptying stadium.

Shakespeare's Coriolanus could not contain his contempt for the ungrateful rabble. The fallen hero eventually goes over to the barbarians and turns on Rome to teach it a lesson. It's been an open secret for weeks: several other clubs are very keen to sign him. Will Abbas drop Sakhnin in its hour of dire need? Will Gumbul's curse become prophecy? Abdullah's deeply pained. But he feels for Abbas. The ungrateful mob has gone too far. Abdullah's pain is Sakhnin's pain: I'm ready to die if only Sakhnin survives.

He's dead serious.

'With God's help'

This Saturday is doomsday. The Sons know they really can't afford to let the town down. Especially because just hours before the final do-or-die fixture in Nazareth, Mayor Abu Shadi — arriving to inspect 'how green is the grass?' — reveals that just before the onset of the Sabbath, the Prime Minister's office confirmed that the missing £4 million needed to complete the stadium is 'in the pipeline'. The whole of Israel knows now that we're here on our ground, that we're an inseparable part of . . .

But today, the rest of Israel doesn't exist, the rest of the world doesn't exist — there's only Sakhnin.

No one in town's on his own. Mahmoud Ghalia's with a group of friends, anxiously drinking coffee. While waiting for the final game of the season, they've been awaiting the news from Jerusalem. Abu Shadi our soul! We leapt as one into the air. It's soon all over town. When soccer's in the air, it takes little for rumours to spread like wildfire. And, this isn't even a rumour. What a good omen! With all that money coming in, we definitely can't afford to lose this final game. Several hours later, Mahmoud and his buddies are still waiting together, wandering together – at Hamoudi's hummus-*nargileh* joint, at the Tora Bora billiard-*nargileh* hall, at Abu Ali's pure hummus joint, at Abu Abdu's, the spanking mod 'Disney' coffee house-*nargileh* hall, just opened at the western gateway to Sakhnin by Yusef Abu Abdu, midfielder in the club management team. One and all, all-men's clubs. Billiard balls click in the rear as a shrieking espresso machine substitutes for the whistling of a shimmering Arabic coffee pot.

How far are you going, Mahmoud? What's happened to you? That far? Mahmoud's wife is looking for him. Last night, Balad, the nationalist Palestinian-Israeli party, staged a political meeting in town. It used to be that Azmi Bishara, the ebullient Balad leader, could be counted on to draw a sizeable crowd in Sakhnin. This time, Azmi draws less than the 35 fans whom Mazen took to Albania. Where were you, Mahmoud? Far from his old stomping grounds – it's not that soccer is killing politics, but that for nearly six decades we've kept faith with politics. Our elected political leaders have failed to secure Arab rights. People reckon politics simply isn't their league any longer. Politics has gone down because soccer is up. It's up even if we go down.

Isn't it Abdullah who always says, what else do we have other than soccer? Abdullah, heart, soul and very being with Bnei Sakhnin; Abdullah, ready to lay down his life for The Sons –

he's proving it brick-by-brick, stand-by-stand, jump-by-jump; Abdullah, the loyal foot soldier – ready for whatever happens this afternoon.

Abdullah's the fourth of seven brothers and two sisters. In the lounge adjacent to Palestine Mosque a family briefing takes place before the end game. The discussion's about Samer, his second oldest brother. Samer's a graduate of Bar Ilan, the religious university in Tel Aviv. He works as a teacher in Beersheba. He's come home for the survive-or-die game. Abdullah doesn't want Samer to risk his reputation on the pitch. At the front, soccer passions sometimes take over, subsume even the purest dreams: it could turn dirty, the chants sometimes become offensive. Samer shouldn't be exposed to the insults, a teacher shouldn't be tainted, he should watch at home, give us his support from home.

Again last night, Abdullah couldn't sleep a wink: At 2am, my friends and I drove down to the beach to wait for the sunrise, to while time away until the 5pm kick-off. A long countdown to the final whistle. Under pressure, a helluva long wait. When Sakhnin's under pressure, everyone's under pressure. This is a national affair – the whole country wants to know: will Sakhnin survive today's crunch game? If it isn't Betar Jerusalem, it's just got to be Ashdod – their second nemesis team this year. National interest aside, it's very much a domestic affair, a score for The Sons of Sakhnin to settle for themselves: With our spirit, with our blood, we redeem you, O Sakhnin! Or, to paraphrase Taysir: Even if we lose, we stay up – till death.

Abdullah knows the score: results from the other besieged teams mean that, despite the agony of the defeat to Hapoel Tel Aviv, the future of The Sons of Sakhnin, the future of their fans and their families, rests entirely on themselves. All they have to do is get all three damned points this afternoon. Never despair.

Ahmad: It's a rubber ball my friends, He plays with us, not us with Him. I'm still on a high from the grass, and you wanna bring me down. No way!

Bilal: First we stay up, with God's help, with our might, by God's might, we stay up, with God's help. Then everything will be 100 per cent okay.

Mahmoud: Are you saying: with – or without God's – help?

Bilal: (*incredulous*) What are you talking about 'with or without God's help'! Without God's help, there's nothing. We came up and we've stayed up – only with God's help.

Mahmoud: Surely, also with the help of the players and the manager?

Tarek: With God, I say. If God doesn't help . . . If God helps, it'll go fine, and we'll stay up with God's help. With-God's-help, for God's sake!

The few in Sakhnin, the paltry few who are not entirely convinced that, at the final whistle, salvation will come courtesy of divine intervention (or of luck, or of superstition, or of conspiracy), offer another explanation – a rational irrational explanation. In *al-Ahli*, Mahmoud calls it 'The Power of *Muammara*'. A well-worked conspiracy, it translates, a fusion of beliefs – in God and in conspiracy, a belief that bridges believers in God with believers in conspiracy. *Muammara,* in Mahmoud's theory, is Sakhnin's unbeatable trump card.

The proof goes like this: the Israeli 'establishment' has belatedly come to the conclusion that 'it's very good for the country to have Sakhnin in the top league'. See the former Prime Minister, Shimon Peres, during a recent visit to our town. Peres was himself facing a threat of relegation from politics. 'Woe unto us all if Sakhnin are relegated', was his message. Q.E.D. See, 'they'll do everything and anything to ensure our survival.'

The high priest of *Muammara* proceeds to another example of how *Muammara* has already worked on the pitch: Abbas's goal is not the only miracle. How many were needed to keep Israel's goalkeeper Dudu Awat's line intact against Ireland? You may scoff, but pray tell what other explanation is there for a ball that goes in and goes out, but doesn't want to go in – not once, not twice, but three times! There's no other rational explanation why Israel was saved from conceding a third, a fourth, and a fifth goal and came away with that miraculous draw. It contrasts with the rational national explanation for the miracle of how Israel was saved – what puny sportswriters who don't see the broader picture call 'the X-factor – the luck of Avram Grant.'

Luck, miracle, superstition or *Muammara* – which of the Four Wonders of the World (according to Sakhnin) will bring Ashdod to its knees? No one wants to believe the result can be otherwise.

The fourth of the five daily prayer times coincides with kick-off. The opening whistle finds several fans still down on their knees in the gangways of the stands. In absence of prayer mats, their heads are bowed onto their Sakhnin scarves spread out neatly on the concrete. Pray to the Prophet! Pray to the Prophet!

One boy, bare-chested, doesn't want to miss the run-on. He offers his prayers from his standing place in block C. Thin arms gyrating, a crane about to take off. He mouths his prayers silently. Then he joins the vocal salute: *Salu an-Nabi*! Pray to the Prophet! A whirling dervish levitating above the players' tunnel. Banners herald the universal power of conviction: Sakhnin won't go down. It's The Word.

'The Word' is actually an anticlimax. Where's the suspense?

Eight minutes into the game an Ashdod defender completely miscues his clearance. Agoye Olomide, who has missed and missed for a month, surely can't miss this time. Can he? He can't. He doesn't. One–nil, Sakhnin.

Relief more than joy. But nerves put to work for so long, a season long, can't be set to rest quite so easily. The game settles into a humdrum pattern. Sakhnin may be winning but, curiously, there's more apprehension than ever. The nightmare scenario: It's a deception. The Sons are sleeping on their laurels and Ashdod are waiting to pounce on the apathy and . . . and . . . and . . . God-forbid-you-know-what. Even the deepest pessimists still can't bring themselves to utter the taboo word – failure.

Heart failure – literally: the second half is just under way when a fan, watching from the steps leading to the upper stands, collapses. A roar goes up. 'The Word' has come true. A replay of Pray to the Prophet! Pray to the Prophet! Abbas! Abbas, down on his knees with a prayer of his own. It's two–nil, Sakhnin. Pray to the Prophet! Pray to the Prophet! Delirium. No flags. But the Sakhnin mast is high. Red-and-white *keffiyehs* and red-and-white scarves are unfurled, flown just like flags. The clamour is deafening. Summoned urgently, a medic somehow manages to make himself heard above the din: An ambulance. Quick! Eyes wide open fight for breath. A few fans breathlessly tear themselves away from the celebrations, help to get him comfortable, raise his feet, fan him with their scarves. Heart attack – where's that stretcher. Another fan comes down from the stands: I'm a doctor. The stretcher arrives. *Salu an-Nabi!* The fan in pain is taken to the waiting ambulance. Abbas is down from the shoulders of his teammates. Still, 39 agonising minutes to survival.

It's all too easy. A perversion of *Muammara* kicks in, snidely crawling into the stands like a nasty rumour. The word now is conspiracy: see, Ashdod want to atone for their original sin of the season and are taking it easy, making it easy for Sakhnin. They won't let Sakhnin go down. You know what, there must've been pressure on Ashdod to atone.

But it isn't easy. We deserve every bit of what we get. The snide rumour is quickly quenched, the conspiracy theory silenced. *Muammara* takes possession. Our belief is strong. We're winning because we believe – in Abbas, in The Sons, in God; 'God is always there'. How can we not give credit where credit is due – to our team?

Conspiracy v *Muammara*. For mid-table Ashdod, either way, the result here today is meaningless.

Still, the archpriest of *Muammara* isn't taking any chances. Just in case, Mahmoud enlists superstition to the cause: Two up. Only five minutes left. But there's still injury time. I'm not standing, I'm not changing my seat, I'm not moving a muscle – else, we may lose. The whole crowd is on its feet: I'm staying put. Mahmoud misses the final whistle, the moment of triumph wasted. But the sacrifice is worthwhile, and those long bloody weeks of agony: You know what, all that while, I never really doubted we'd survive.

Everyone's mobbing everyone – Ghazal and Abu Shadi, Ibrahim and Hilmi, Gumbul and Abdullah, Alain Massoudi and Momi Za'afaran, Mundar and his cigarettes, Mahmoud and everyone, Abbas and just about everyone, Mazen and my-brothers-the-cops. If this party is just about securing tenth spot in the league, just about escaping relegation, what happens when they win the league?

Bilal: We've stayed up!

Ahmad: Thanks to all Sakhnin fans!

Bilal: Sakhnin my soul!

Ahmad: Sakhnin on the map forever!

Bilal: The Arabs stay in the National League! All the Jews and their teams play us again next year!

Ahmad: Another season, another year.

Tarek: Let's not get carried away. Soccer isn't everything. Okay, we won today. But at most, we've forced a draw. If you think we're ever going to get into their league, forget it.

Right, it's only soccer. Mundar is hoarse from chain-smoking his way through the 90 minutes. His mind is clear, though, about everything that's happened this season. And what lies ahead: We say over and over – look beyond the soccer, to partnership in this country, to success in that partnership, to being partners in success, not partners in failure. Some Jewish citizens still stereotype us. The Abbas goal has changed some hearts. Still, sometimes we have to swallow hard, sometimes we hold our tongues. But we have a platform for change. Right, we're not yet in the top league – in Israel's League of Acceptance. Yet, slowly, slowly, one goal at a time, you create trust, help forge a sense of community, of shared interests. More and more are willing to accept us. Now, we're settled in the league and we'll go on winning hearts. Eventually, we'll have equality. That's the winning goal.

It's close to midnight on this warm early summer night. Abbas has finally managed to escape the crowds. All over town, ever since the team returned home from their temporary home near Nazareth, there's been a non-stop celebration, dancing in the streets and fireworks. The 20-mile journey back was one giant procession, a replay of that Cup night exactly a year ago, punctured by joyous rallies at junctions leading to other Galilee towns and villages.

In the Suan compound, a huge weight has fallen away from the four three-storey buildings. The concrete soccer pitch in between has become the stands. Those who weren't in Nazareth gathered in a semicircle of plastic chairs around the TV pitch to watch the triumph. And when darkness falls, floodlights from the roofs create an illusion that the compound is the real pitch. Courtesy of Sakhnin's pirate TV channel, Neptune, the Suans watch themselves triumphant in a non-stop replay of the highlight of the day. In the informal women's section of the stands, fervent thanks to God: '*Ya Rab, Ya Rab, Ya Rab*'.

Abbas is greeted with a nice cup of tea, neighbours pop in to wish him, the family and themselves a hearty *mabruk* (congrats). He signs autographs (in Arabic and Hebrew) on postcards which carry his picture with the national team. The question – over and over: What's more important – winning the State Cup last year, or staying in the league today? Opinion is divided. But the Abbas family have no doubt. Abbas, Safa and Said Hamad are in full agreement: the moment of the season was neither. It was the moment when Abbas saved Israel. Since that fatal goal, as glory gave way to pressure, as Bnei Sakhnin faced impending doom, as the town faced relegation, father and wife quietly shared the burden of a hero devoid of even a moment's grace. They seethed with a captain questioned by his own faithful: You cannot imagine how great the pressure was, as if my boy carried The Sons alone. Fortunately, Abbas has broad shoulders. Safa never lost faith in him: Self-belief – if we've learnt anything, we've learnt one thing all this season, that if you're strong, and show strength to your opponents, they come to believe in your strength. They respect you. And, you in turn, believe in yourself. With every good reason – next season, on our own ground . . . in Sakhnin.

Chapter 14

'We too Have no Other Land'

Piece of cake

ALL SEASON LONG, almost every day, Hamzeh Bros. have taken an order from at least one family in town to bake a birthday cake in the shape of a football ground. We make a new ground every day! The motto of Walid Hamzeh of *Halawiyat Walid Hamzeh*, Sakhnin's favourite confectionery. No one's unhappy that their favourite line (the other is a Grand Prix racing circuit) is soon to be discontinued. The dream cake's finally coming true. Soon, the stadium-starved children of this never soccer-satiated town will have 'the real thing'. They'll no longer need to settle for ersatz. Soon, the real stuff will replace the figurines set into the green icing, the studs of the players' boots biting into the newly laid turf, making their mark, and replacing the teeth marks of the young fans biting into the marzipan.

And the bride will wear green

At the 'real thing', the mood is buoyant. An oven in the baking sunshine. Work is at a feverish tempo. Abdullah's back at his regular day post, hammering nails into the new South Stand: Next season, next season. The South Stand is where Abdullah will sit with Gumbul, Hilmi and all the boys of The Sons. Over there, we've already completed the West Stand which will host our visitors. What! Abandon the west side that was traditionally the boys' home stand – historically, our place? Don't the most dedicated deserve the best view that you get in a side-on stand? Abdullah's gracious: That's reserved for our guests. They'll be alongside the VIP stand. We'll take the new stand here behind the goal. All season long, we've been wandering. We made friends, in Tel Aviv, in Haifa, in Ashdod, even in Jerusalem. The time has come for Tel Aviv, Haifa, Ashdod, even Jerusalem, for everyone, to follow their teams here. We want them to feel at home.

It's the finishing phase. Abdullah's hammer and pliers are subbing for his jackhammer, trowel and mortar. Sakhnin, *olé, olé.* Up, up, still in the top league, in the top league, yet another season, yet another year. Look how clever my nails are. They have no heads. Nothing can ply us out. We're here to stay. One ground, one league forever.

The word is that the necessary funds have finally been banked. The Master of the Ground and the Master of the Stands can proceed with the floodlighting – the last critical phase in this 'national project par excellence'. The Master of the Turf waxes eloquent: You're looking at the bride preparing to don all her finery for the wedding party. We're about to dress her in the bridal gown. Some powder, a touch of eye-liner, an extra dab of rouge here and there, a sprinkling of rosewater – she'll be tip-top for her big day.

Only one small detail: the date for the dedication ceremony of the palace of dreams has still to be set. An 'ill-advised source' in City Hall suggested the first of October. That's hardly a date for a celebration – it's the commemoration of the killing of The Thirteen. It's inconceivable to have a memorial and a soccer festival on the same day, says a 'well-advised source' in City Hall. The mayor arbitrates between his 'advising sources': The question needs to be carefully examined from every angle. I shall soon convene a steering committee. Make a note, Ms Wafiqa, would you please tell Ghazal to set up a meeting at Abu Ali's.

There's a jaunty air about the stark 160-foot extended arm of the giant crane that's been contracted from a Tel Aviv company to lift the slabs of concrete on to what promises to be the liveliest part of the ground – Abdullah's Stand. Resplendent in black-and-red, the crane needs to be gigantic for the herculean task. The little piece of machinery costs a trifle more than the 15 x 10 inch, 10 pound cake available at Hamzeh Bros. The cost of the crane: around half-a-million pounds, just under a quarter of the cost of the entire renovation project of the 105 x 68 metre 'real thing'.

A Gulliver in Lilliput perched high up in the cab of his crane, Moti Trinti takes a break from the lifting job. A giant weightlifter manoeuvring a giant with his fingertips, he loves every minute of it: They give you such respect here – this stadium means so much to the people here. It's such an honour to do it for them. Moti's a fan of Maccabi Haifa, the champions, and favourites again next season. But he's already a confirmed fan of the ground: No matter my loyalty to Haifa, I'm committed to be here for their first home game. Each time Moti drops another heavy slab from heaven, another heavy weight falls from Abdullah's shoulders. Just a couple of weeks ago, he was genuinely worried that the declared deadline wouldn't be met and that his nomadic wanderings would continue far into next season.

Down to earth, two of Moti's Lilliputian assistants (Boris originally from Kazakhstan and Llona from Moldova) take a far less lofty view. Llona sniffs: You'd think we've never built a stadium before – 4,500 seats. It's routine. Boris and Llona do concede there's 'something special' in this project – the small metal loops thoughtfully installed by the Master of the Stands that respond to a simple swift twist of the wrist. That allows them to detach the giant slabs easily as they're lowered from the crane: Piece of cake. We have to admit, that's class service.

Class and commitment is what drives the Master of the Stands. Still, he's pressed by the Master of Turf: You make a promise, you have to deliver. Don't you worry about my stands, you look after your turf, make sure it's greener on your side of the fence. My game-plan is carefully calculated, I look back to where I was when you were just putting in the first clumps of turf and I know we can do it. Don't forget to mow the lawn neatly. The people of Sakhnin are expecting it.

Expecting and inspecting. A steady procession of pilgrims, fathers and sons togged out in red and white, stream in. Farouk Zubeidat confesses he's making his third pilgrimage since ten this morning: I'm here to monitor how far progress has progressed. The *muezzin* has yet to issue the call to noonday prayer from Palestine Mosque that towers over the West Stand. At 11.30, we were all pleased to see that they'd begun mowing the grass. I just hope they won't mow down our dreams. Farouk gets an approving nod from headmaster Abu Majdi. Most of the pitch pilgrims make a detailed examination of the edge of the grass. All carefully keep a respectful distance and avoid treading on the hallowed lawn. No need for 'Keep off the Grass' signs. Abu Majdi chuckles. He remembers Abu Shadi's promise on Lawn Day – no 'No-Go' zones here. This is self-imposed No-Go. The shadows from a flock of doves circling above the crane for a bird's eye view are the only trespassers permitted on the turf. The headmaster gives another approving nod.

Suddenly, Abu Shadi materialises from behind the Wadi Safa End: I have an important announcement. Gather round. Pilgrims, workers, Masters all gather round expectantly: I hope we'll make the deadline. I hope we'll be able to make it. The mayor beams broadly, but stonewalls all further inquiries. A heavy slab descends on poor Abdullah. A wild rumour is instantly ignited: They're running out of funds, they're running out of funds. More of a crowd gathers. The buzz now is no longer of expectation, but of suspicion. Pilgrim-in-Chief Farouk pleads: I told you so. I told you I was worried they might mow our dreams. I'm sure they've got the money. It's just the mentality of this country – to weep crocodile tears about having no money. Money? There's plenty – Thank God! Poor Abdullah's lost: I don't get it, I don't get it – we're not going to be able to complete the ground? I was hoping we could already begin to book our seats.

Abu Shadi heads back to his car. Belatedly, he realises that his 'important announcement' hasn't exactly hit the target in the way he'd planned. To offset the rumour he himself has helped create about how much money there is in the ground kitty, Abu

Shadi convenes an emergency meeting behind the South Stand. He instructs Master of the Stadium and Master of the Stands to boost their crews to double strength. And to put on double shifts. He sets off a new rumour: Does the mayor have something up his sleeve? What's behind that cherubic smile? I'm telling you, they like to mow our dreams. Abu Shadi's just toying with us. It's the national addiction to pressure. I keep telling you that this is a nation hooked on getting things done at the 90th minute. The Pilgrim-in-Chief almost steps on the holy lawn in anger, and in total disregard of the invisible 'No-Trespassing' signs. Abu Majdi shakes his head in disapproval.

Pressure, like last-gasp goals – nothing better calculated to get the adrenalin going. So, will we have our ground, or not? Abdullah's convincing himself it's better to believe that we'll have our ground – and that it will be ready, as planned, for the wedding day, the opening home encounter at the start of the new season – even if we have to work long into the dark, as late as midnight.

All that remains is the not-so-little matter of the invitations to the wedding party. Ms Wafiqa has duly passed on Abu Shadi's message to Ghazal and at Abu Ali's, Town Hall's favourite hummus hang-out. The steering committee is in session. Like for any wedding, getting the invitations absolutely right, and also the seating order spot on, can make or break a glorious send-off, even if a firm date has yet to be set.

Ghazal: The Prime Minister – he's a certainty. After all, he's the No.1 supporter of our Ground.

Abu Ali: I'm pencilling him in.

Abu Shadi: Abu Mazen (Mahmoud Abbas) I reckon too.

Ghazal: Absolutely. He should be a certainty too.

Abu Ali: I'm pencilling him in too.

Abu Shadi: What about the new Minister of the Interior?

Abu Ali: Should I put him down already?

Ghazal: Hang on a sec. Let's think it through.

Abu Shadi: Put him down as a sub meanwhile.

Ghazal: Then, what about the Palestinian Interior Minister?

Abu Shadi: Right, isn't he originally from down the road in Beit Shean? After all, that was our home for several games this season.

Ghazal: You got all that, Abu Ali? He got all that Abu Ali.

Abu Ali: So whom am I pencilling in now?

Of new alliances and new friendships

For the past few days, even the greenness of the turf has been supplanted as the talk of the town. At wedding parties, in hummus joints, billiard halls and *nargileh* parlours, in family courtyards, and at all four corner-flags, the talk is of one thing and one thing alone: the quiet disclosure that the Emirate of Qatar is to donate 'at least $10 million' to expand the stadium, and to redefine Sakhnin as Galilee's 'Sports City'. It's going to be renamed 'Doha Stadium'. Aha – now, it's coming out, that's the great news Abu Shadi had been so anxious to share with the Wadi Safa End – all he wanted to tell about funds for the stadium but was unable to disclose (because of the sensitivity of this 'historic agreement'). Mindful of the caution from Sakhnin fans to their opponents – 'Shut up and be quiet, you maniacs!' – Abu Shadi duly kept his mouth shut. The mayor had been so wary about revealing his Qatari connection that he scored an own goal. He couldn't brag about his historic achievement, the very first investment by an Arab state in an Israeli town. Abu Shadi's still wary because some might still regard this connection as unwholesome, as unholy.

But, why all of a sudden, Qatar? Why now? Is this *Muammara* at work? What accounts for the Qatari munificence? It begs for insights from Mahmoud: Who cares the reason! How long have we been yearning for the Arab world to stop cursing us for staying on our land in 1948, and instead begin to embrace us precisely because we were steadfast – because we stayed, literally held our ground? How long until they begin to understand our predicament? You want to tell me honestly that, with politics alone, without the Cup, without the goal of Abbas-My-Soul, without the crowning of Abbas as the saviour of Israel – we would have gotten support from the State of Israel and from an Arab state at one and the same time? And you want to tell me that the colour of *Muammara* is not green? Every blade of grass in our 'Doha Stadium' is a little *Muammara*.

Abu Shadi warms to his role as soccer diplomat. He casts the Qatari largesse as backing for Israeli soccer as a whole as much as support for the Arabs in Israel. After all, like the fans always say: Don't we play in the Israeli premier league, didn't we lift Israel's State Cup? A subtle diplomat this Abu Shadi: Lachman and Mazen could have learnt a wily tactic or two.

A state for all its supporters

Is my son's cake ready yet, Walid?

Wurrod is at Hamzeh Bros. to pick up a ground-cake for the birthday party of her five-year-old boy, Amir. Last-minute preparations, Walid sprinkles ground-up Aleppo pistachio nuts on the white-icing cover of the chocolate cake: If only our ground was as green as this one. It's his fourth stadium of the day: Sakhnin are red-and-white. We have the ball. Here's Abbas. He places the No.8 sugar-coated figurine just outside the Chantilly cream penalty area: He's going to score. G-O-A-L! *Yalla yalla ya Sakhnin!* – the Pavlovian cry from Walid's teammates behind the *knafeh* counter. That doesn't move Wurrod. She teaches standard three. She knows all about childish behaviour: That far, Walid! I know you're going to tell me we have nothing in Sakhnin other than soccer.

Until this afternoon, when Wurrod spoke of nothing matters in Sakhnin but soccer, she meant the rest of the town. When she spoke of The Sons besotted with soccer, she meant all the sons of town, but not hers. This afternoon, her family's joining the club: When they come here to play in Sakhnin, maybe the ground will help them understand that we were born here too, that we didn't fall out of the sky, that we exist here.

What should I write on the ground?

Just put 'Happy Birthday Amir' – he's five today. Oh, and also, 'Happy New Season'. You know what, write down: 'Bnei Sakhnin 5, Betar Jerusalem 0!'

Loads of creamy benedictions are instantly squeezed from the Chantilly tube. Coloured sugar sprinkles thrown onto the grass, confetti raining down on the stadium because of the latest thumping of Betar.

Yalla yalla ya Sakhnin – from behind the cash register.

Thanks, *shebab*, lovely. Let the ground be a symbol to all the people of Israel that we're here, that all our families are here, that our sons are here. Amir will want to keep it forever. Bye, *shebab*.

Wurrod puts the cake carefully on the seat next to her and drives the ground home – around the corner and up the hill.

She climbs the stairs and is almost knocked over by the team of five-year-olds warming up for the party kick-off. Happy birthday, they sing and dance, Beautiful sweet season!

She turns on the six floodlights – five for his birthday, the sixth for his next season. Blow them all out Amir. The chant from the family stand: Happy birthday, Beautiful sweet season! All out at one go, well done!

G-O-A-L! A slurpy kiss for Amir from elder brother Ahmad. No. 1 fan Wurrod lifts the new No. 5 high into the air. A big hug for Amir-My-Soul.

She cuts the ground cake: Would that we all rejoice in our lives here, in peace! That will be a winning future.

The children line up. Wurrod hands them each a plate: My dream is that my children will want to stay here, that they'll be happiest here, that they'll grow up in peace, with love in their hearts, that they won't tell me one day, 'we're leaving', that they'll feel that this is the finest place on earth. We all need to accept the truth about this land: Two teams on one ground, two people – Arabs of Israel and Jews of Israel – in Israel.

'We too have no other land'

'I Have No Other Land' is a popular Hebrew song from the time of Israel's first war in Lebanon. A sad peace song composed in time of war, a song of pain, a song sung by people yearning for better times, a sentimental song that, like a drop of water onto a rock, slowly cleaves into the Israeli psyche, a song that Jewish

Israelis like to sing together on their turf, from their home stand, a song with the aura of a secular hymn, a hymn to the comfort of having a home:

I have no other land
Even if my land is aflame
Just a Hebrew word pierces
My veins,
My soul –
With an aching body,
With a hungry heart,
This is my home.

Words and lyrics: Ehud Manor, 1982

Wurrod brushes off the remaining crumbs: We too have no other land. Would that everyone on both teams be ready to unite and embrace that! Then we both – Arabs of Israel and Jews of Israel – could stand together on the whole ground before every match and sing together: We have no other land. Home sweet home, land sweet land!

The children remove the plastic goals and players and put them on the fast-emptying tray.

Final minutes of the Steering Committee

Abu Shadi: So, now we're all clear on who's coming. But what are we inviting them to?

Ghazal: He's right you know – nobody's going to come just for the opening of a little soccer ground. I know what'll make them come. Everybody loves a winner. Let's say on the invitation: Come to the home of Bnei Sakhnin – Israel's perennial soccer champs.

Abu Shadi: Brilliant! And when we've convinced them of that, they'll come to see The Galilee Games in Doha Sport City – the volleyball, for instance!

Ghazal: Volleyball? Since when is volleyball our game? Volleyball's a luxury.

Abu Ali: Volleyball?

Abu Shadi: Explain it to him, Ghazal.

Ghazal: Didn't you hear what George Bush said about Israeli politics? He called it, 'Israel's national contact sport'. It's like karate, he said, you never know when the next chop will come.

Abu Ali: So?

Ghazal: You still don't get it: Volleyball, unlike karate or soccer, is a luxury. There's no interaction, absolutely no contact with your opponents. Interaction, that's our game, that's the Sakhnin game!

Abu Ali: So, should I also pencil Bush in?

Extra Time

The Cup in the Cupboard

AND SO IT CAME TO pass in the land of Galilee that one of the goals had been met. They had finally settled on the date of the first real home game, the first game of the new season. It came and went without much fanfare. The Sons lost. Actually, they got whacked, three-nil. Good that none of the big-wigs actually came, though the modest opening ceremony did go off fairly well. You could even be forgiven for thinking that now that they have a ground, why do they need a team at all? At least, when they didn't have a ground, they won their 'home' games.

Every football stadium has its own trophy cabinet to show off their triumphs and to brush away their traumas. The puzzle — what has happened to the Cup? It was paraded round the town and country. One of the paparazzi captured the trophy curled up in bed in Abbas's arms. After that it simply vanished.

Some thought the mystery disappearance was just a ruse so that

Sakhnin could keep it forever and not return it to the FA at the end of the season. Floating trophies are always supposed to be returned, aren't they? Tradition must be maintained. It was claimed that someone among The Sons' management put out the story that in those celebratory wanderings from village to village, and here all around town from household to household, it had simply 'got lost'. Lost? You've got to be kidding! The Sons lose the Cup! They'd lose their minds, they'd exchange jerseys with Betar, but they'd never lose the Cup. They'd even be prepared to lose to Betar rather than lose the Cup.

The reason was more prosaic – and more romantic.

Mazen has finally explained the mystery. He confides how he'd had to respond to so many offers, entreaties, demands, pleas from fans that he let the trophy take pride of place, night after night, on a different mantelpiece so that they too could bask in the glory of briefly hugging it. The mundane truth is that the Cup was battered out of shape because of too much love, too much adoration, too much adulation. When the chairman realised what had been done, he was just too embarrassed to give back a bruised and broken cup.

Still, Mazen couldn't sleep from worry. Perhaps someone in the FA would say: See, you can never trust Arabs, give them something to treasure and they'll ruin it! He could hardly have told them the truth: the big bump, the unwholesome boil on the left curve, the twisted neck, the crushed crown sitting at a jaunty angle. Definitely, it didn't befit the dignity of the State Cup. So Mazen decided to tell the FA that the Cup was lost, pure and simple, and would be replaced. So the Cup remains hidden in Mazen's cupboard, occasionally brought out into the light for a quick spit-and-polish.

The Cup in the Cupboard

In the cupboard, out of the cupboard, in the dark, in the light, a season comes, and a season goes. A time for everything in its own season, so they say, though that particular Biblical wisdom about a time for killing and a time for healing and a time for breaking down and a time for building up – like the one guy who applied the Bible literally and took the whole of the season to break down the stadium in order to build it up again – doesn't apply to a soccer season, because everyone knows that in the world of soccer there's no time for anything else but winning.

Even with the new stadium, things are pretty much the same in Sakhnin. Sure, a few things have happened: a war with Hezbollah in Lebanon which saw hundreds of missiles fall on the Galilee, a peace conference and a few peace gatherings, more fighting and yet more fighting. Life goes on. Abbas's dream of reaching the World Cup Finals did not happen. Even with Arab players scoring goals, Israel never made it to Germany and it's doubtful that they'll get through South Africa. *La-Rachnah wala-Chaynah* – literally, we didn't leave and we didn't live: same old same.

And Betar's nasty chants too, though there was one memorable time (no more than a brief interlude, mind) when again they abused the Prophet's memory and actually got punished for it, though it turned out to be not even an interlude, since in no time the punishment was reduced. Some even blamed The Sons for starting it all just by being around to challenge Betar in the first place. See, nothing's changed.

As for The Sons, they've had their ups and downs – they've been down and now they're up again. Back in the top league and doing better than ever, though you still find yourself wondering whether that old 'survive at all costs' genie has been shelved and locked away with the battered Cup. The club's got a whole bunch of solid foreigners now and Meir Cohen, the goalie, is not only Jewish, he's the captain. You could say that The Sons have totally sobered up and have had enough drinking from the glory of the Cup. Now, they're playing soccer *netto*, they're politically carefree, dedicated to winning on the league pitch, no longer committed to the bombast of winning on the national pitch. It's easy to understand why the guy from the shop up Martyrs' Street just a few doors from where the Cup was hidden in Mazen's place – you know the shop where, alongside the jerseys, the scarves and all the other football paraphernalia – says, let's pray we don't win that damn Cup again. Once in a lifetime's enough. You don't want to challenge them too hard. All we want is to be normal, just like the Jews.

What else has changed? There are those coloured signposts hailing 'Doha Stadium' dotted all along 805. Abbas has moved on, wandering to a series of new clubs. He doesn't need directions when he comes back home to play as a visitor. Whenever he plays in 'Doha' with his adopted team, he's applauded sportingly. And, sportingly, he's never scored at 'home'. So, you could certainly call it an honourable draw, though a draw isn't the sort of result that ever satisfies any true fan. You certainly can't win a cup that way. Why need a cup if you play for a draw?